TEACHING ADULTS

A 2014 GED® Test Resource Book

Developed by ProLiteracy

New Readers Press®
ProLiteracy's publishing division

Acknowledgments

Thanks to Chris Richards for his help and advice in creating this book. Thanks to Annie Holden and Christina Williams Saulter for providing valuable feedback and guidance. Thanks to Kathleen Ruddy and the adult learners at the Sisters of Notre Dame Legacy Project for their participation and field testing.

Thanks to Amy Vickers, Heather Indelicato, Danielle Legault, and Heather Turngren of Minneapolis Adult Education Center.

Special thanks to Linda Church and Katie Bova for their help and expertise.

And thanks to Martin Kehe, Vice President of Products at GED Testing Service for reviewing the information about the 2014 GED® test.

Teaching Adults: A 2014 GED® Test Resource Book
ISBN 978-1-56420-472-1

Copyright © 2013
New Readers Press
ProLiteracy's Publishing Division
104 Marcellus Street, Syracuse, New York 13204
www.newreaderspress.com

Printed in the United States of America
9   8   7   6   5   4   3

Proceeds from the sale of New Readers Press materials support professional development, training, and technical assistance programs of ProLiteracy that benefit local literacy programs in the U.S. and around the globe.

Writer: Meagen Farrell
Developmental Editor: Terrie Lipke
Associate Director of Marketing and Communications: James P. Wallace
Technology Specialist: Maryellen Casey
Designer: Carolyn Wallace

GED® Test Assessment Targets, Extended Response Scoring Rubrics, Webb's Depth of Knowledge, and screenshots courtesy of GED Testing Service.

Contents

Introduction

This Book

Teaching Adults: A 2014 GED® Resource Book is a guide to the new test and how to prepare your students for it. This book contains descriptions and details of the test as well as strategies and activities to use in the GED test-preparation classroom.

Chapter 2 provides an overview of the test. Chapter 3 provides information about working with adult GED students. Chapter 4 describes the use of an interdisciplinary instructional approach with GED students and offers some interdisciplinary activities for classroom use.

Chapters 5, 6, 7, and 8 take a deep dive into the requirements for each of the four content-area tests. In addition to describing each test, the chapters also include activities. Chapter 9 covers digital literacy, the computer skills required for the new test, and activities to familiarize students with the computer skills required for the test.

Appendices include detailed descriptions of test requirements, reproducible graphic organizers, and sample lessons.

ProLiteracy

ProLiteracy, a nonprofit organization based in Syracuse, New York, champions the power of literacy to improve the lives of adults and their families, communities, and societies. It works with adult new readers and learners and with local and national organizations to help adults gain the reading, writing, math, computer, and English language skills they need to be successful. ProLiteracy advocates on behalf of adult learners and the programs that serve them, provides training and professional development, and publishes materials used in adult literacy and basic education instruction. It has 1,100 member programs in all 50 states and the District of Columbia, and it works with 50 partners in 34 developing countries. ProLiteracy was created in 2002 through the merger of Laubach Literacy International and Literacy Volunteers of America, Inc. ProLiteracy's publishing division, New Readers Press, publishes materials used by literacy instructors and programs.

Find out more about ProLiteracy and how you can become a member at www.proliteracy.org. To look at the New Readers Press online catalog, go to www.newreaderspress.com.

For More Help: ProLiteracy Education Network

ProLiteracy has a special website for tutors, teachers, and program managers who are working with adult literacy or ESL (English as a second language) learners. The site is called ProLiteracy Education Network or simply EdNet. It contains free online professional development courses and other resources designed to help you improve the services you provide. ProLiteracy continues to add new resources to this site, so plan to visit frequently. You can access it at www.ProLiteracyEdNet.org.

The GED® Test

History

The GED test offers an opportunity for people to demonstrate they have developed skills equivalent to those of a high school graduate. To date, more than 18.7 million individuals have passed the GED® test. Over the years since its inception, the test has changed, as have the reasons that people take the test.

G.E.D. originally stood for General Educational Development. The American Council on Education (ACE) developed the GED test in 1942. As the U.S. entered World War II, the military requested a standardized assessment to measure the skills of veterans who had not completed high school and wanted to continue their education. The test was mainly used by colleges to determine whether people had the level of knowledge required for admissions. Veterans also used the GED test as a credential to enter the workforce after returning home. After a few years, ACE made the test available to the U.S. public.

GED Testing Service® (GEDTS) has revised the test several times to keep pace with changes in education and the economy. The 1978 test series introduced real-life contexts and reading materials while test items shifted from recollection of facts to application of conceptual knowledge. The 1988 test series featured the addition of the written essay and also emphasized critical thinking and problem solving. These changes were made when it became clear that more people were taking the test to enter postsecondary education than to apply for entry-level jobs.

The fourth test series was released in 2002 and reflected the latest high school content standards. Since then, people have been taking the GED test to get entry-level jobs, to advance in their careers, to begin career training, and to apply for postsecondary education. All 50 states and the District of Columbia use 2002 GED test results in order to issue high school equivalency diplomas. In addition, 98 percent of colleges and universities and 96 percent of employers accept the GED test credential as equivalent to a high school diploma on applications. The test is now administered in all 50 states, U.S. provinces, Canada, and in various locations around the world.

The 2002 GED test series consisted of five subject area tests: Reading, Writing, Math, Science, and Social Studies. The entire test took a little more than seven hours to complete. Though originally a paper-and-pencil test, it has been making the transition to computer. By the end of 2013, most states are slated to offer this test on computer at authorized GED testing centers. This paves the way for the new computer-based assessment to be released in January 2014.

The 2014 GED test series will include four subject area tests: Reasoning through Language Arts (RLA), Mathematical Reasoning, Science, and Social Studies. Total test time will be about seven hours. As before, test-takers may take the four tests separately, in any order, or all at once.

The GED test credential is not a diploma. It is a standard measure of skills used by state jurisdictions to issue a high school equivalency credential. This distinction is important because the new 2014 GED test will not be the only high school equivalency assessment available. States may offer other assessments instead of or in addition to the GED test. Two such alternative tests are the Test Assessing Secondary Completion (TASC) from McGraw-Hill and the High School Equivalency Test (HiSET) from Educational Testing Service (ETS).

The 2014 GED Test

In response to the movement toward the development of national college- and career-readiness standards, ACE began to rethink the purpose and development of the GED test. In 2011, ACE joined with Pearson VUE® to create the new GED Testing Service, LLC. With an eye toward the future, GEDTS began work on the new 2014 GED test series which will debut on January 2, 2014.

> NOTE: Check the GEDTS website regularly for updated information on all the following topics. www.GEDTestingService.com

What Does the Test Look Like?

Following are some major changes that guided GEDTS in developing the new test.

Standards-Based. GEDTS wanted the assessment to measure the knowledge and skills adults need in order to be successful in careers and in postsecondary education. To that end, they relied on widely accepted standards when developing the assessment targets. The assessment targets describe the skills and knowledge that the GED test measures. The Common Core State Standards (CCSS), College and Career Readiness (CCR) anchor standards, Texas College and Career Readiness

Standards, Virginia Standards of Learning, The National Research Council's Framework for K-12 Science Education, the National Curriculum Standards for Social Studies, and the National Standards for History were used to develop the assessment targets.

Forthcoming national assessments and curricula will likely reference the CCSS as a common language. To date, 45 states, the District of Columbia, four territories, and the Department of Defense Education Activity have adopted the math and language arts standards that were developed for use with K-12 students.

While not aligned solely to the CCSS, the new test will be impacted by the changes that the CCSS signify. For instance, CCSS sets higher expectations for reading comprehension and thinking skills in grades K-12. For more information about CCSS, see www.corestandards.org. See Appendix A for lists of specific skills that people are expected to have and topics they are expected to be familiar with in order to pass the GED test.

Depth of Knowledge. On the 2002 GED test, Bloom's Taxonomy guided item development by defining levels of activity required to complete tasks. In contrast, the 2014 test uses Webb's Depth of Knowledge (DOK) which focuses on the complexity of the cognitive processes adults use to perform those activities. The DOK consists of four levels:

Level 1: Recall – Tasks require recall or recognition of skills or behaviors.

GED test example – Recall the sequence of events in a reading passage.

Level 2: Skill/concept – Tasks require mental processing beyond recall or recognition, such as using information or making decisions. Tasks entail more than one mental or cognitive process.

GED test example – Summarize the main events in a reading passage.

Level 3: Strategic thinking – Tasks require reasoning, analysis, and deep understanding of content, for example, problem solving and drawing conclusions. Tasks may have more than one possible answer or may require justification for an answer.

GED test example – Analyze the dialogue between two characters in a reading passage, and describe the interaction using evidence from the text.

Level 4: Extended thinking – Tasks require the integration of knowledge from multiple sources and usually involve work over an extended length of time.

GED test example – No test items will require level 4 thinking.

Since the new test emphasizes higher order thinking skills, GEDTS used DOK to help develop test items that require mental processing or reasoning skills at mainly levels two and three. Only about 20 percent of the test items will require level one DOK, 80 percent will require levels two and three, and no items will require level four. This focus on critical thinking skills means that test-takers will be expected to plan, use evidence, and make decisions about how to approach problems.

For more information about DOK and the GED test, go to www.gedtestingservice.com/exploring-the-2014-ged-test-webinar-archive.

Computer-Based. Beginning in January 2014, the GED test will be delivered and managed on computers at authorized testing centers. Only those centers that have met the requirements to become Pearson VUE® Authorized Test Centers will be able to receive and offer the new test. It is important to note that although the test will be on computer, it is not Internet-based. Testing centers will download the test onto computers, and test-takers will not be connected to the Internet during testing. The test is also not adaptive. In other words, test items do not increase or decrease in difficulty depending on test-takers' answers.

In addition to answering multiple-choice items, test-takers will need to respond to a variety of technology-enhanced item types. These items will require test-takers to type a response (e.g., fill-in-the-blank, short answer, and extended response), drag and drop answers to the correct place, select answers from drop-down menus embedded within text, and manipulate hot-spot items with sensors (e.g., plot a point on a graph). See Chapters 5–8 for details on the types of items on each test. See Chapter 9: Easing into Technology for more information on the digital skills required.

Three versions of each subject area test will be available the first year, allowing for two retakes. More versions may become available over time. The switch to a computer-based test means that updates and adaptations will be easier to implement. New or revised test items can be added at any time. The GEDTS intends to conduct periodic norming studies so that it can revise the test to align with changes that occur as K-12 standards evolve.

Test-takers who are unable to take a computerized test due to disability must fill out an Accommodations Request form and follow the Documentation Guidelines for Candidates found at www.gedtestingservice.com/accommodations. See Chapter 3: Teaching Adults for more information on accommodations.

Official Practice Test. Late in 2013, a half-length, electronic readiness test will be released. GED Ready™ will be available for purchase through New Readers Press and other GED test preparation publishers. GED Ready will give test-takers firsthand experience answering computer-based questions modeled on actual GED test items. Instant electronic score reports will identify areas of strengths and weaknesses and link to publishers' materials to help you create study plans for students.

Interdisciplinary Assessment. Reading and writing are combined on the new RLA Test. Literacy and quantitative reasoning will be assessed in context across all four sections. With the addition of constructed response items, writing will be assessed across three of the four tests:

- Two short answer items on the Science Test will require a brief, typed response. Answer length is expected to be a few sentences or a paragraph. The suggested time for this task is 10 minutes.

- Two extended response items will require test-takers to read and analyze multiple passages and/or graphic stimuli and respond to a prompt.

  ▸ One 45-minute extended response prompt will appear on the RLA Test.

  ▸ One 25-minute extended response prompt will appear on the Social Studies Test.

The four content areas will often overlap. For example, test-takers might have to demonstrate reading comprehension skills on a science passage or use math calculations to answer a social studies question. You will find more details on the content of each test in Chapters 5–8.

Varied Item Format. The change to a computer-based test allows for more variety in question formats. In that way, the test can measure more complex skills and concepts and also allow people to demonstrate basic computer skills. The computer-based item formats also allow for quick scoring by computer.

Test-takers need to be able to use the mouse, do basic keyboarding, and use some directional tools to answer questions. The chart shows item types, which test they will appear on, a description of how they work, examples of test items, and how they are scored.

Passage Sets and Item Scenarios. Multiple items that refer to a single stimulus are grouped in passage sets or item scenarios. The RLA Test comprises text passages of 400–900 words followed by six to eight test items. The Math, Science, and Social Studies Tests comprise discrete items as well as item scenarios which may include two or three items with a single stimulus, such as brief text, graphs, tables, or other graphic representations. The Social Studies Test may also include maps.

Navigation. Navigating the test requires basic computer skills: mouse clicking and scrolling. A split screen display allows test-takers to see passages and/or graphics alongside questions. Scrolling may be required to see some passages and graphics. Longer passages will be divided into pages with numbered tabs. Test-takers will be able to "flip" the pages by clicking on the tabs.

Test-takers will also be able to navigate from question to question, backward or forward. The item number will be displayed at the top of the screen. "Previous" and "Next" arrows at the bottom of the screen can be used to move from question to question.

Item Type	Description	Examples	Scoring
Multiple choice (Tests: RLA, Math, Science, Social Studies)	Use the mouse to click and select the correct answer from four choices.	Similar to questions on 2002 test, but only four answer options.	1 point each
Drag and drop (Tests: RLA, Math, Science, Social Studies)	Click on an item and drag it to the correct place.	Drag numbers and numerical expressions to assemble an equation. Drag words or phrases into a graphic organizer to compare, categorize, or sequence. Drag items to maps or graphs.	1 point each
Hot spot (Tests: Math, Science, Social Studies)	Click on items that have virtual sensors in order to select answers or select the placement of an item.	Click items to select multiple answers. Click on a graph or map to indicate the correct placement of an item, such as a point or place.	1 point each
Drop-down (Tests: RLA, Math, Science, Social Studies)	Click to select the answer from a drop-down menu.	Choose the correct sentence from a drop-down menu embedded within a text passage to demonstrate editing skills on the RLA Test. Choose a word, phrase, or numerical expression to complete a passage or equation on the Social Studies or Math Test.	1 point each
Fill-in-the-blank (Tests: RLA, Math, Science, Social Studies)	Type a number, word, or phrase into an answer box.	Type a word, phrase, or number to complete a statement or answer a question.	1 point each
Short answer (Test: Science)	Type a few sentences or a paragraph in response to a prompt based on a text passage or graphic stimulus.	Write a summary, conclusion, or hypothesis. Cite text evidence to support a conclusion.	3 points max May be scored holistically or awarded 1 point for each part of a multiple-part answer.
Extended response (Tests: RLA, Social Studies)	Type a written response to a prompt that is based on one or more text passages.	RLA: 45-minute task SS: 25-minute task Read and analyze source text(s). Type a response to the prompt that includes a thesis statement and an argument that supports the thesis and uses evidence cited from the text(s).	RLA: 12 points max SS: 8 points max Both will be scored using three-trait rubrics.

TEACHING ADULTS: A GED® TEST RESOURCE BOOK

If a test-taker is unsure about a question and wants to revisit it later, he or she can "flag for review." Clicking on the flag icon at the top of the page marks a question with a flag. At the end of the test, an item review screen will list flagged and unanswered questions so that the test-taker may return to them.

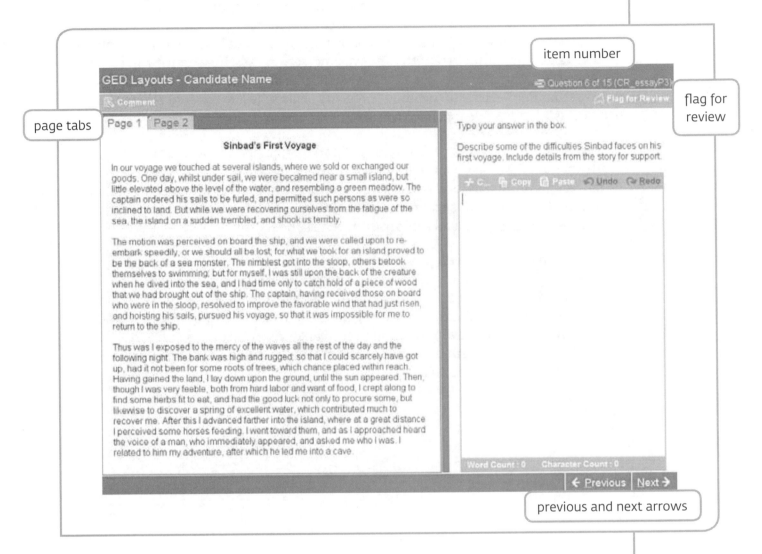

item number

flag for review

page tabs

previous and next arrows

Multiple Formats. The new GED Test will also be available in Spanish and Braille. A JAWS screen reader version will be available for test-takers who need audio support.

Other Changes

Registration and Scheduling. Test-takers will be able to locate the nearest testing center, register, and schedule a test online at any time. They will also pay online with a credit card or voucher. Price may vary by jurisdiction, so check with your local test center for the price in your area. Test-takers will need an email address to register since registration confirmation and scores will be sent to this address. To locate the nearest testing center, enter your location at www.gedtestingservice.com/testers/locate-a-testing-center. The website for test registration is www.GEDcomputer.com. For more information on the online registration process, see Chapter 9.

Scoring. According to the GEDTS, the percentage of test-takers planning to continue their education has increased to nearly 64 percent. In response, the new test has been developed to measure career and college readiness as well as high school equivalency. The score report will provide qualitative feedback about test-takers' academic strengths and weaknesses. The testing service will conduct longitudinal studies over the first few years of test operation to validate the score level that demonstrates the knowledge and skills required for test-takers to be successful in first-year college courses.

Test scores for each of the four tests will range from about 100 to 200 points. The passing level score for high school equivalency will be 150. To pass the entire battery, a minimum total score of 600 and an average score of 150 per test will be required. The test will be standardized and normed using a representative sample of graduating high school seniors from across the nation.

An automated scoring engine will score the tests and will email scores to test-takers within three hours of test completion. Even the short- and extended-response items will be scored by computer. Each short response item will have specific answer requirements. Scoring guides and exemplars will be developed by humans and used to train the computer to analyze and score the responses. If an extended response item is flagged by the scoring engine to be scored by a person, the score report may be delayed.

Teaching Adults

Motivating Adults to Come to Class

GED test-prep classes are not all alike. You may teach a large class, a small group, or one to one. Your program may include volunteer tutors, paid instructors, or a combination. One challenge for instructors in any of these situations is motivating students to continue to come to class. The first thing you need to remember is that GED students are adults. They are busy people who probably have family and work obligations. They have come to your class to achieve an important goal. As an instructor, you need to understand their motivations and how you can help them not just to pass the GED test but also to succeed with their goals.

Here are some ideas that you can use to help motivate students to come to class:

- show tangible progress toward goals,

- support learner confidence,

- develop a learning community,

- help learners to build supportive personal networks, and

- make class relevant.

Show Tangible Progress toward Goals

For some adult learners, passing the test is their only goal. They may be so focused on getting their GED credential that you have to continually relate what they're learning to that goal in order to help them progress. For others, it may be what that diploma means that really matters. They may need to pass the GED test to get a job or a promotion. They may want to pass to get a high school diploma and set an example for their own children. Each student will have his or her own reasons and goals.

When you meet new students, ask what their goals are. If a goal seems difficult or like it will take a long time to achieve, work with the student to break it into several short-term goals. Capture these goals on paper or in an electronic file that you can return to frequently. Check in at regular intervals, and be sure to acknowledge when a goal has been achieved. That way the student will be able to see progress along the way and stay motivated.

Sometimes you can use the indicators in the back of this book to help you do that. Show the plan to the student and make a point of checking it regularly. For example, suppose you have a student who says, "I need to pass the GED Math Test. I'm pretty good with numbers, but I'm terrible at geometry and algebra."

Long-term Goal: To pass the GED Math Test

A. Short-term goal: Master geometry

   1. Learn to use a hand-held calculator for basic functions.

   2. Learn to use an online calculator for the same functions.

   3. Learn the basic terms related to shapes and to geometry: square, triangle, rectangle, polygon, trapezoid, area, perimeter, radius, circumference, volume.

   4. Compute the area and perimeter of triangles and rectangles.

   5. Compute the area and circumference of circles.

   6. Compute the perimeter and area of a polygon.

   7. Compute the perimeter and area of composite geometric figures.

   8. Memorize the formulas that will not be on the math formula sheet.

   9. Identify how you would use this information to solve problems in your daily life or at work.

B. Short-term goal: Master algebra

Be prepared to explain to students how a lesson or activity relates to their goals. They may not see the value in activities that don't seem directly related to their lives. Showing students how their day-to-day lessons connect with their long-term goals or relate to their lives will help them to be engaged in class.

Consider this example: A woman enters the class because she wants to open a day care center. She thinks it will help if she gets her high school equivalency diploma. In addition to clearly stating the skills she will be learning and telling her about the progress she makes in doing that (see above), you need to make sure to relate what she is learning to her ultimate career goal.

Example

Skill	Application to goal
Compute the perimeter of a rectangle.	Figure out how many yards of fencing are needed to make the yard safe.
Use ratios to convert units of measure.	Calculate the amount of each ingredient to use if changing a recipe that feeds 4 to one that can feed 15.
Calculate volume of a rectangular box.	Figure out how many bags of sand to purchase to fill a sandbox.

Students in GED classes may have had negative experiences in school. So it's important to acknowledge their previous knowledge and experience as well as recognize progress. Provide plenty of opportunities for students to practice new skills, and offer positive feedback when they demonstrate new skills or reach interim goals.

Support Learner Confidence

Sometimes adult students are insecure about their ability to learn. This may come from having had a bad experience in previous schools or from negative interactions with teachers, prospective employers, family members, or even peers. There are many ways that you can support your students and help them to gain confidence in their own abilities and capabilities.

Here are some suggestions that may help you to build your students' trust in you, the class, and in their own learning:

- Offer frequent praise and support: Acknowledge and celebrate every goal and milestone. With each accomplishment, learners will build confidence to strive toward new goals.

- Emphasize previous experience and knowledge: In today's world, everyday experiences and street smarts count! Students may not realize how much they already know. When you begin work on a topic, be sure to ask what they already know about it. Acknowledge any skills or information that relate to the lesson. If a student remembers something about the topic that is incorrect, give him credit for contributing, and explain that as he explores the lesson he might learn things that change his mind.

- Be open to learning what students can teach you. This is another way to acknowledge previous experience. Get to know the learners and ask them to show or describe to you and their classmates a skill that they have. This is a great get-to-know-you activity as well as an opportunity to praise students for their existing skills.

- Design instructional activities that relate to students' work, community, family, hobbies, or interests. Not only does this engage learners, but it also provides an opportunity for them to participate by telling what they already know.

- Use guided practice to build confidence. Students may need lots of practice before they can demonstrate certain skills on their own. Use a gradual, scaffolded instructional process to teach the skill, allow guided practice, and then gradually offer opportunities for students to demonstrate the skill on their own. Some students will need more practice or more guidance with some skills. Be patient. Break skills into small bits, and provide support as students learn each bit. Then as they learn and build confidence, gradually allow them to complete tasks on their own. Praise their accomplishments.

- Don't put learners on the spot. If you know that a student is not comfortable with a topic yet or still needs guidance, don't put her on the spot by asking a question in class that she is not able to answer correctly. It's better to ask a student who is confident of her answer. That will give the confident learner a chance to showcase his knowledge, and listening to the answer will give others an opportunity to learn from their peer.

In general, get to know the students. Offer opportunities for them to succeed, and praise them often for their accomplishments. By making your classroom a place where they feel supported and comfortable, you allow them to become confident learners.

Develop a Learning Community

One way to bring together a class of disparate individuals and help motivate them to come to class is to develop a learning community. If you have a group of students who are working toward a common goal, they can help and motivate each other. Make sure that students feel that they can participate in class without fear of being criticized or ridiculed. Set rules for the classroom that will help all students feel safe and respected.

Each classroom is a micro-society with its own culture. As the instructor, you help set the tone for the classroom, but you are not the only source of learning. Students also learn through observation, experience, and interaction with everything around them. You can motivate and engage students by developing a community that accepts them, encourages them to learn and explore, and helps them reach their goals.

Instructors can intentionally develop an inclusive learning community using icebreakers and team-building activities. These interactions will help students get to know each other and to feel comfortable talking to each other. Some students may even offer to lead icebreakers. Here are a few ideas to get you started:

- Ask students to share their names and answer a question. Sample questions:

  ▷ Why do you want to pass the GED test?

  ▷ What do you do to keep focused on your studies?

- I'm a fruit, you're a fruit (or geometric object, animal, etc):

  ▷ Ask each student to introduce himself to one other student and tell that student what fruit he is.

  ▷ Get the whole group together in a circle.

  ▷ Have each student introduce another student by telling his name and his fruit.

- The line game:

  ▷ Put a line of masking tape on the floor and ask everyone to stand on the line.

  ▷ Make a statement and ask everyone who agrees with the statement to stay on the line. Ask those who disagree to step off the line. (Sample statements: I have worked in a factory; I have children; I drive a car; etc.)

  ▷ Try to end with a statement that everyone can agree with.

- Remember the facts:

  ▷ Arrange students in a line or a circle.

  ▷ Have the first student say her name and a fact about herself.

  ▷ Have the next person in line say his name and a fact about himself and also to restate the name and fact of the person before him.

  ▷ To make this more challenging, have students recall the two people before them or everyone who went before them.

- Agree or disagree?

  ▷ Post each of these words in a different part of the room: *Definitely Agree, Agree, Neither Agree Nor Disagree, Disagree, Strongly Disagree.*

  ▷ Ask a subjective question, and ask learners to stand next to the sign that shows how they feel. (Sample questions: I like pizza; I would vote to reelect the president; I think children should go to school year-round; etc.)

▷ Ask students at different stations to explain their answers.

- Name-gesture game:

  ▷ Arrange students in a line or a circle.

  ▷ Have the first student say her name and make a gesture (for example, wave hand, put a finger on the nose, tug an earlobe, etc.).

  ▷ Have the next person in line say her name and make a gesture and also to restate the name and make the gesture of the person before her.

  ▷ Challenge yourself to be last and to remember everyone's names and gestures.

Clear expectations for class participation provide support for those students with low social skills or motivation. Increased responsibilities and clear leadership roles can help learners who demonstrate higher levels of social skills and motivation.

Here are some suggestions for things adult learners can do that will help them to engage and participate more fully in the GED classroom and with each other:

- Develop and agree on rules for class discussion or other classroom rules and routines

- Make or bring snacks and beverages

- Investigate and report on local learning resources, such as libraries, tax preparation services, immigration resources, etc.

- Learn the names of and some basic information about other learners and program staff members

- Exchange contact information and initiate or participate in communication outside of the classroom, such as email addresses, phone numbers for calling or texting, or social networks. (Let students decide if they want to participate. This should be voluntary.)

- Suggest or discuss and agree on learning topics of interest

- Volunteer to act as peer mentors to help others learn a particular skill, such as computer skills, setting up email accounts, or other skills they may be willing to share

- Help organize class events such as recognition or graduation ceremonies

- Represent the class or program at local events or offer to be interviewed for local media

Help Learners to Build Supportive Personal Networks

Another factor that can motivate students not just to come to class but also to stick with a program is a network of supportive friends and family. Students need support not just for motivation, but also to help manage their obligations at home, at work, and at school. A study on persistence reported that "the strongest positive force mentioned by adult students was the support of people, particularly their families, friends, teacher, and fellow students." (Comings, Parrella, Soricone, 1999)

Encourage students to create a support system that includes not only people who can help with day-to-day needs like child care or transportation to class, but also people who can serve as successful role models. If a student doesn't know someone who has been an adult student or attained a GED credential, provide opportunities for him to meet successful students from your program. Invite previous students to come in and talk to your class about their experiences in preparing for and taking the GED test. It's important for students to see that their goals are attainable and to be able to visualize their own success.

Make Class Relevant

One way to ensure that students want to attend class is to make it relevant to their lives. It's probably not possible to link every test topic to real life, but the more often you can tie lessons to your students' needs, the more engaged they will be. The next section will talk more about how you can do this even if you are using commercial GED test prep materials. Chapter 4: Using an Interdisciplinary Approach also talks about ways that you can use students' ideas to enhance your lesson plans.

Relating GED Test Prep to Real Life

Some people use test-prep materials to study for the GED test. Some take practice tests, and some study with a "big book" that covers all the content on the test. This kind of focused, repetitive practice works for some people, but not for everyone. Adults who work exclusively with test-prep materials may get bored quickly. Most of these materials don't relate the content to real-life experiences, so some learners may have difficulty understanding why they need to learn or remember the information.

Even when using these materials, you can still find ways to connect your instruction to real-world experiences and to the individual goals and needs of your students. When you do this, the benefits reach beyond the test. You will help students transfer their newly acquired skills to everyday life.

Think about pre-school or kindergarten classes: How do children learn at this age? They may act out different roles, play with blocks and puzzles, or take care of a class pet. Early childhood educators know that young children learn first through the real world. They teach children using concrete, real-life examples—things that they can see, touch, and manipulate.

All students, whether they are adults or children, benefit from learning with things they can touch and see. For example, you may be working on geometry problems where students need to figure out the area of a rectangle. You can activate memory and integrate multisensory learning by asking students to identify concrete examples of how they can use this process in their everyday lives. Maybe they need to figure how much carpet or paint they will need for a room they are remodeling. Maybe they need to figure out how many brownies they can get out of one pan. Maybe they are planting a garden or fencing a yard. Students can suggest scenarios and come up with their own examples of area problems. Then they can work on these problems individually, in pairs, or in small groups.

Some adult education programs use contextualized instruction to relate skills students learn in class to skills they will use in everyday life. Contextualized instruction means "using the content of parenting, life skills, job training, and/ or civic participation to teach literacy and higher order thinking skills in the context in which they will be used. This means there is a clear connection between the goals of the learner and the instructional strategies." (Texas Center for the Advancement of Literacy & Learning)

Example: Using contextualized instruction to teach reading comprehension skills

Reading target / *indicator*	Content	Context	Application
R.6 Determine the author's purpose or point of view in a text and explain how it is conveyed and shapes the content and style of a text.	Parenting	Two articles written by authors with differing viewpoints on whether or not childhood MMR vaccines can cause autism.	Discuss the two points of view and use the discussion to make a list of questions you would want to be sure to ask your pediatrician.
R.6.1 Determine an author's point of view or purpose of a text.	Job/career	Two articles written by authors with different points of view on what the impacts will be if the minimum wage is increased.	Discuss the two points of view and decide what position you would recommend that your union take on this issue.

Get to know your students—their goals, their jobs, and their needs. Take advantage of situations where you can connect a learning objective to a student's life. Ask students how they might use a new skill at home or at work. Then you can create practice scenarios that are based on real-world application. The more real your lessons are to students, the more likely they are to be engaged and to remember what they learn.

Building Self-Advocacy Skills

What is self-advocacy? Self-advocacy is "an individual's ability to effectively communicate, convey, negotiate, or assert his or her own interests, desires, needs, and rights. It involves making informed decisions and taking responsibility for those decisions." (VanReusen et al., 1994)

You probably won't have time to teach your students all the skills they need for all the situations they may encounter or decisions they will have to make, but you can keep this in mind when you work on lesson plans. For example, when you discuss making an argument or citing evidence to defend a position, introduce some real-world examples. Ask students if they have ever had to apply for help after a natural disaster, report damage to an insurance company after a car accident, or report a crime to the police. Discuss how being able to tell or show actual evidence helps to support a claim. You also may want to discuss the importance of describing an event in detail, in the order that things happened. These are important life skills that you can directly relate to your lessons.

Nowadays, to make a reasoned argument people need much more than just words to tell a story. In the 21st century, U.S. residents who seek help or compensation for health problems, crime, work conflicts, or natural disasters can make a more compelling case by using detailed narratives, graphs, maps, receipts, forms, diagrams, and other types of evidence.

Especially in science and social studies, GED instruction can go beyond teaching about graphs, diagrams, and political cartoons using GED prep materials. Adults can practice these skills by using their own experiences, challenges, or interests. For example, a learner with the goal of attending college could graph his savings plan to predict when he will have enough for tuition. A learner could create a family diagram to track the instances of a serious medical issue. And a learner could get a deeper understanding of editorial cartoons by illustrating her own viewpoint on a controversial issue in her community.

Encouraging Learner Engagement and Independent Learning

Many adults like to be involved in the decisions about what and how you teach. When learners are the center of instruction, they take ownership of their learning. Learners can take part in planning instruction by

- setting goals,
- selecting activities, and
- choosing materials,
- evaluating the lessons.

When adult learners are involved in the decision making, they are more engaged in the instruction. This type of involvement can also help students transition to independent learning. That may mean doing homework outside of class, reading on their own time, taking online courses, working independently in a computer lab, or seeking advice from a friend or neighbor who has expertise in the learner's area of interest.

To encourage learners to participate in decision making, solicit their feedback. At the end of each class or lesson, ask students what they liked, what they didn't like, and what they would like to know more about. Use the feedback to plan future lessons. If students did not respond well to a topic, but it's an important one, then try to find an approach that will help them relate to it or that might pique their interest and make them want to know more.

If they liked a topic or wanted to know more about it, you can do extension activities or plan a lesson that goes into more depth. For instance, if you have been reading literature, maybe a student is curious to know more about the author. If you are calculating probability, maybe a student would like to know how to calculate probable outcomes in a favorite game. These are ideas that you can use to foster independent learning. Help the learners to locate information or set up problems that they can read and practice on their own.

Another way to make instruction more learner-centered is to let the students be in charge of their own assessment. Many test-prep materials include assessment tests and practice tests. You can also use the official GED practice test: GED Ready. Adults can take and score these assessments on their own. After they see what items they get wrong, you can help them to make a plan for studying and practicing those topics.

Not all learners will want to or be ready to take charge of their own learning, but guiding them in that direction will give them skills that they can use for a lifetime.

Tools

Learners who know what they need to find out can be taught how to use available tools to locate and evaluate new information themselves. A simple example of this is when a learner realizes she has encountered a word she doesn't understand, and she looks up the definition in a dictionary. When learners take the initiative to find information and answer their own questions, this not only saves class time but also encourages independent learning. Several activities in this book involve using or creating common tools to organize, find, and retain information. Look for opportunities within your lessons to facilitate and allow students to practice using tools on their own.

The computer-based GED test has several tools available to test-takers. Students will benefit from practice with the TI-30XS calculator—whether virtual or handheld. They should also become familiar with the calculator reference sheet, how to access it, and what's on it. It may reassure nervous test-takers to know that they can refer to it during the test. The math formula sheet and symbol selector are also available to students. Talk to students about tools that they use at home, school, or work. And encourage them to use tools.

Managing an Adult-Ed Classroom

What can you do to manage a class with students who have different goals, are at various levels, and can come and go when they want? Here are some suggestions that may help:

1. Break up a large class into small groups or pairs: You can group students working at the same level so that they can learn together or you can pair a low-level student with a higher-level student. The students can work together and help each other to complete a project or an assignment.

2. Utilize peer teaching: Peer teaching can be can be very motivational for learners. Consider occasionally asking a more advanced student to work with a group of lower-level students. This works especially well if the students can relate to each other through shared goals or similar experiences. Maybe you can ask a student who has recently passed the GED test to volunteer in your class. This offers students a role model and a real-life example of what their success may look like. Remember that your advanced students will want to work on their own goals, too, so don't become dependent on this.

3. Hire or contract with a counselor: If you have a counselor available, students will be able to discuss personal issues privately, rather than in class. A counselor can offer help with situations that interfere with study time and also refer students to programs that can help with problems like transportation or childcare.

4. Use volunteers or paid aides: Having help in the classroom ensures that you will be able to give all your students the attention they need. Tell students that you are all on the same team, and that you, your aides, and all of the other students are there to help them succeed. You are building a learning community.

5. Establish a computer lab: Students who need basic computer skills can benefit from learning and practicing on computers not just for the GED test, but also for jobs or further study. Pair a student who is comfortable with the computer with another who needs to learn to use it. You can also have students who do have basic computer skills work independently on the computer while you address a different topic with other students.

Easing into Technology

Starting in 2014, the GED test will be delivered exclusively on the computer. Students who are not comfortable using a mouse, navigating on-screen information, and typing on a keyboard must master these skills before they take the test. The computer skills required for the test are similar to those needed to browse the Internet, use word processing software, and complete digital forms.

Students should practice answering questions and writing essays on the computer before they take the GED test. The more comfortable they are performing tasks on the computer, the better they will do on the test. The first thing students will need to know and to practice is how to navigate through the test items, access the available tools, and read the necessary texts and graphics.

The GEDTS has tutorials on its website that guide students through the process of registering for the test, scheduling a date to take the test, and taking the test on the computer. Currently, these tutorials simulate the actual process that students will need to follow in order to take the computer-based 2002 test. Soon the tutorials will be updated to reflect the skills and tasks required for the 2014 test.

There are also tutorials that students can use to practice navigating the test items and answering the computerized questions. Students should practice using all of the available features, like flagging questions for review, even if they think they might not use them. Tell students that they should be prepared to use every feature so that they have the best chance to succeed on the test.

There are many ways to help students practice using the technology, features, and item types on the new test. For example, students can practice navigation just by entering websites, scrolling up and down pages, and clicking to open new windows. Students can also prepare for using the on-screen calculator by first using the handheld version of the TI-30XS. Print out the calculator reference sheet and review it with students. Tell them that they will be able to refer to this sheet on-screen during the test. After they get a feel for how the calculator works, they can use the video tutorial on the GEDTS website to practice the types of calculations they will do on the test.

Students should also review the math formula sheet and the Symbol Selector. The more familiar students are with these tools, the easier it will be for them to use them during the test. For more details about the Math Test, see Chapter 6.

Computerizing the GED test has many advantages. Adaptive technology will be used to accommodate some learners with disabilities by enlarging text, using a text reader, or changing the display contrast, for example. Test-takers will benefit from the quick feedback they will get after the test. Automated scoring makes it possible for test-takers to receive scores and detailed information about their strengths and weaknesses within three hours of completing the test. Technological advancements also save time and administrative costs. The test will be easier to update and revise, so future changes may be in the form of incremental updates instead of major transformations.

We can automate assessment, but we can never automate genuine communication between human beings. As an instructor, you may not have control over the changes that new technologies are bringing to your classroom. However, you do have control over how you use the new tools and how you present them to your students. Some of your students are probably excited about and ready to try a computer-based test. But others may resist giving up their pencils and paper. You can motivate reluctant students by modeling computer use in the classroom.

Ease students into using technology by helping them to set up free email accounts. Even if they only use email in the classroom to send assignments to you, they are still getting practice with keyboarding skills. Be sure to present opportunities for students to practice keyboarding skills in preparation for the extended response items.

Encourage students to do online extension activities, such as reading more about a lesson topic on a website. This will help prepare them to navigate the test and read the stimulus passages. Access the tools and tutorials on the GEDTS website to help students become familiar with the look and feel of the new test. Supplement print materials with online practice. You will be preparing students not just for success on the new test but also for the technology they may encounter at work or at school. You will find some activities in Chapter 9: Digital Literacy.

Using Accommodations

We don't know exactly how many people have learning disabilities (LD), but it's possible that some of your students do. In fact, 40 percent of students with LD drop out of high school without a general diploma (National Center for Learning Disabilities, 2011). In addition, adults with physical disabilities and chronic physical or mental health problems sometimes drop out of school for similar reasons—they don't get the help that they need.

What can you do? Some adult students may have been diagnosed, but many have not. If you suspect that one of your students has a learning disability, speak to your program director and seek professional help. Only a professional qualified to do a formal assessment can give an actual diagnosis.

Older students may have hearing or vision problems. Often you can accommodate these students in your classroom by speaking loudly and clearly or by enlarging text on a computer screen.

To create an accessible learning environment, present information in various formats so that students can process the information in whichever way works best for them. Here are some tips for making classroom instruction more accessible:

1. Use visuals, audios, and movements to reinforce learning for all three senses. Some of the activities in this book can be multisensory. For example, you could use Activity 21: Pros and Cons Graphic Organizer. Make a T-chart on the board or the wall. After discussing the topic and writing it at the top of the chart, have students write their pros and cons on sticky notes. They can place the notes on the chart where they belong.

2. Use captioning or a text transcript with videos. Some videos have a closed-caption option that you can turn on. The National Center on Disability and Access to Education offers information and resources that may help you to produce and/or use accessible videos at www.ncdae.org.

3. Use technology. Many textbooks are available in electronic format, which can be enlarged or read aloud with a text reader. Explore alternatives that may be available to your students, and try them yourself. Then you will be prepared to help your students.

4. Coordinate with other organizations. Learners with very specific or multiple disabilities may need more assistance than your organization can reasonably provide. You may need to contact a specialized organization for advice and support. Be sure to get the student's consent before sharing any protected information about health or disability status.

Test-takers can request a variety of accommodations for the GED test. Familiarize yourself with the options, as well as the request forms, so that you can help students who need them. If students will be using accommodations, have them practice with similar methods in class and when taking practice tests so that they will be comfortable during the test. For detailed documentation guidelines, FAQs, accommodations request forms, step-by-step directions, and information for evaluators, go to www.gedtestingservice.com/accommodations.

Here are some of the accommodations that test-takers can request on the 2014 test series:

- Extra time (25%, 50%, 100%)

- Extra "stop-the-clock" breaks

- Large print or screen magnification

- Paper test

- Auditory presentation

- Braille

- Color and contrast options

- Plug-and-play adaptive equipment

- Separate room

- Reader/recorder

- Talking calculator

Other customized solutions may be available. Contact GEDTS to find out more. It may take up to 30 days, or longer for complex cases, for accommodations to be approved.

In order to apply for test accommodations, a licensed diagnostician must complete parts of the request form. The chief examiner at your local testing center or your state's GED test office may be able to offer referrals or help filling out the forms.

Using an Interdisciplinary Approach

As mentioned in Chapter 2, the new GED test uses an interdisciplinary approach. What does this mean for test-prep instruction? In cross-training, athletes train in several sports in order to improve overall fitness. Interdisciplinary or cross-curricular instruction is like cross-training that connects or integrates lessons on a variety of subjects in order to facilitate critical thinking and a deeper understanding of the material. Interdisciplinary instruction also teaches new skills in contexts that are relevant to the learners. The ultimate goal of this kind of instruction is to prepare learners for real life, not just for a test.

Integrated Instruction

An interdisciplinary approach to GED instruction means integrating skills and knowledge from more than one discipline or subject area to solve problems. Although each of the four subject-area GED tests has its own focus (such as math), the GED test developers created items that intentionally assess more than one subject at a time. For example, RLA focuses on reading, but 75 percent of the readings are nonfiction passages—some with science and social studies content. Writing skills are checked in three of the tests. Test-takers will write two short-answer responses on the Science Test, and they will write an extended response based on a social studies passage. Mathematical reasoning will be assessed within the Science and Social Studies Test contexts as well as the Math Test. Students preparing for the GED test must learn to use reading, writing, and math skills across subjects.

An interdisciplinary approach helps build connections across topics. These connections increase motivation and improve learning (Resnick, 1989; Thaiss, 1986). The four tests also have a strong focus on reasoning skills, which is a way of assessing a person's ability to use critical thinking to process information and solve a variety of problems.

Contextualized Learning

In addition to a focus on integration of various skills in each lesson the new GED classroom will have a stronger emphasis on contextualized instruction. Teachers will plan how to introduce and practice skills within contexts relevant to the learners in the class.

For example, instead of focusing on the isolated skill of solving single-variable algebraic equations, a teacher might have students use this skill to figure out how to get the best deal at their neighborhood grocery store. Or in a lesson on sequence, learners may write a recipe for their favorite food that involves describing the step-by-step process of preparing and assembling ingredients.

By embedding instruction in contexts that are meaningful to the students, a teacher recognizes the importance of building on prior knowledge—what the students already know. As James Zull (2002) says, "Prior knowledge is the beginning of new knowledge." Learning is easier when learners can connect new skills or concepts to something they already know.

Planning Instruction

In planning interdisciplinary instruction, you can choose to organize around themes, essential questions, or group projects.

Themes. The GED test uses themes like "the great American conversation" to connect passage sets and item scenarios that test a learner's ability to meet a variety of assessment targets. For example, on the Social Studies Test, there may be a set of three questions based on a history passage coupled with a graph. Test-takers will need to read and understand the text and graph, and then answer questions that require skills in reading comprehension, comparison and contrast of graphic data, and math calculations. Although the three questions test distinct skills, they are tied together by the theme of the stimulus passage and graph.

In their classes teachers might choose themes of interest to learners that are related to a work or life issue. For example, if a learner wants to get a job in landscaping, the teacher might suggest that as a theme. She can then teach geometry skills by having learners calculate the perimeter or area of a garden in order to determine how many yards of fencing or bags of mulch will be needed.

Here is an illustration of how you can use an interdisciplinary approach while you are covering an Earth science unit on the theme of renewable energy resources.

Example:

Subject: Earth Science	Lesson Theme: Renewable vs. nonrenewable energy sources
Science	Read about energy resources and compare: How are renewable sources different from nonrenewable sources? Activity: Make a chart or diagram that shows the types of energy you use every day.
RLA	What would you do? Write a letter to your congressperson advocating the use of one renewable energy source for your area. Explain why your city should invest in developing that source and what the advantages would be.
Math	Make a pie chart to compare use of renewable and nonrenewable resources in the U.S. Review percentages and how pie charts represent them.
Social Studies	What natural energy sources are available in your area? How does the geography and climate of your state relate to the energy sources used? What are the advantages and disadvantages of the most commonly used fuels?

Essential Questions. Another approach to interdisciplinary instruction is to organize instruction around an essential question. Essential questions are thought-provoking, relevant to learners' lives, and stimulate discussion and debate. In tough economic times a school board often has to make painful choices on how to cut budgets—whether to eliminate some classes, cut back after-school activities, postpone maintenance and construction needs, or lay off staff. These are often of high interest to adults who have children in the schools. For those adults, an essential question might be: "How can we cut the school budget and still ensure that our children get a quality education?" *How* and *why* questions stimulate critical thinking and discussion. There is often no one answer that everyone will agree on. The teacher begins by finding out what the learners already know or think. Then she teaches any key background information about the topic, such as what the current budget looks like, whether students have been improving in reading and math, and how many learners participate in athletics. When learners demonstrate understanding of the information, ask the question again. Find out what else learners want to know and discuss how to get that information. As they learn more about the topic, learners will begin to think more critically about their answers, which may change as they acquire new information.

Knowing your learners' interests may help you formulate essential questions that will inspire them to think critically about the answer and engage in the lessons. Think about what interests them outside class: earning a living, finding housing, maintaining relationships, and enjoying activities or entertainment. Here is an example of how one instructor used an essential question to connect interdisciplinary subtopics:

How can we cut the school budget and still ensure that our children get a quality education?	

| Create a pie chart showing categories of spending. | Percentages: Work with percentages and figure out how much school tax a homeowner pays. | Writing assignment: Write a letter to your school board suggesting how the budget could be cut and explaining why; cite evidence from pie chart. | Budget discussion: Where do school funds come from and what has been happening to the tax base in the community? |

Here are some other examples that could be used as essential questions if the learners are interested in the topic:

- How do you decide what food is good for you and your family to eat?
  - ▷ Nutrition: Bring in food labels and discuss nutrition facts.
  - ▷ Math: Calculate serving sizes, percentages, and quantities.
  - ▷ Technology: Research diet, nutrition, and food information on www.usda.gov.
  - ▷ Global: Where does the food you eat come from? Map the sources of your family's food. Discuss local food movement. What fresh foods are available where you live?
  - ▷ Science: Genetically modified foods—What are they, and am I eating them?

- What is trash?

- Is life better with technology?

- What values are celebrated by your family or your community? How?

- What is safe shelter? How do you secure shelter for you and your family?

- What holidays and historical moments do you celebrate? How?

- How do you participate in government decision-making? What issues are important to you?

- Are statistics always true?

- How do you define success?

- What makes a historical event important?

When selecting an essential question, find out what issues are important to the learners. But be sensitive to learners' cultures when bringing up personal topics like religion or money. Some people may not be comfortable discussing these things in a large group. Also, make sure that learners respect each other during class discussions.

Group Projects. Another way to organize interdisciplinary instruction is to focus on a project. Learners can work together as a class or in small groups to complete a project. A good project is one that has a clear process and outcome. Just like themes and essential questions, a project should be something that learners find interesting and relevant. Successful project-based learning allows students some flexibility in determining what the project looks like and also creativity in how to proceed with the project.

The example below illustrates a simple project for a lesson on graphs. Learners will work in small groups of five or six. This project is adapted from Activity 44: Graph a Text. This activity uses mainly math skills, but you could adapt it to include other topics, such as writing a compare-and-contrast essay based on the graphs or collecting data from the whole class on where they were born and mapping the locations.

Project Steps	Sample Project: Graph Your Lives
1. What question, problem, or prompt defines the project?	What does your group look like?
2. Write a clear description of the expected process and project outcome.	Select, collect, and display data about your group using two of the following: a table, a histogram, a pie chart, a line graph, or a scatter plot.
3. Make a time line.	Tuesday: Decide on what data to collect (15 minutes), collect data (15 minutes), discuss and decide on display types (30 minutes). Wednesday: Create displays (60 minutes). Thursday: Present displays to class.
4. List the skills/strategies that learners will have to use to complete the project.	• Collaboration: Discuss and decide on which data to collect. • Communication: Collect data such as age, height, color of hair or eyes, family size, etc • Critical thinking: Analyze selected data and discuss to choose the best method for display. • Collaboration: Discuss and agree on the display method and design table/graph/chart. • Abstracting problems: Create data display.

Project Steps	Sample Project: Graph Your Lives
5. Describe the process for review and revision of the final project.	Review the tables/graphs/charts you have created: • Does the display method you used show the data in the best way? • Is each table/graph/chart accurate? • Is there any way to improve the data displays?
6. Make a plan for using, demonstrating, disseminating, or displaying the final project.	Present your tables/graphs/charts to the class. Describe the data findings and how the display methods you chose work to show the similarities and differences in the data. Discuss how the data from each group are similar or different.

Project-based lessons can be good ways to engage learners, promote collaboration, and connect topics to concrete, real-world experience. Small projects can be completed within one class period, while larger projects may be done over time or even outside of class. Projects can be based on learner interests, lesson topics, or ideas that arise from discussions about your community.

Making a Published Curriculum Interdisciplinary

If your GED program uses a predetermined curriculum or set of materials, you can still create interdisciplinary lessons. For instance, a teacher could look through the materials and think about how to tie lessons together under a single theme as described earlier. Selecting a theme of how economic development affects the environment and quality of life might allow a teacher to pair a social studies lesson on the Industrial Revolution with a science lesson on the causes of climate change. The teacher could also use math and graphs to look at how temperatures have changed and to predict future temperature changes.

Teachers can also choose to supplement the curriculum with outside materials that address specific learner needs or interests. Discuss the topic you will be teaching with your learners. Find out what they already know about it and what interests them. Discuss how the topic relates to their lives, their jobs, or their community. Then use your learners' ideas to look for supplementary materials—to make the content of the prepared curriculum relate to the learners in the class. Your goal is to find a way to keep learners engaged, promote critical thinking skills, and facilitate understanding of the material they need to learn for the test.

The learners can help by suggesting websites, articles, application forms, or other real-world materials that might relate to the topic. For example, as you introduce a lesson on political campaigns, you may discover that most learners are not registered to vote or have never voted. That's a perfect opportunity to help them learn how to register. Print or display the National Mail Voter Registration Form.

Model filling out the form, and discuss how the questions on the form relate to the voting process. (Why are you asked to choose a political party? Why are you asked about your race? Do you have to answer these questions?)

Whether you are using a prescribed curriculum or creating all your lessons from scratch, you can find many ways to use an interdisciplinary approach to teaching. The more you can do this in class, the better prepared the learners will be to pass the GED test and to solve the problems they face in everyday life.

Activity 1

Discussion: Setting Rules

PURPOSE

To avoid and resolve conflict during group discussion by creating a clear set of expectations.

METHOD

1. Ask the group, "Why are we learning as a group? What do you learn from discussion?"

2. Propose and/or solicit rules for group discussion, for example:

    a. One person talks at a time.

    b. Everyone does not have to agree.

    c. Every person can share her thoughts and feelings.

    d. Respond to the topic, not to each other's comments.

3. Ask the group if they are satisfied with the list of rules. "Does anyone want to change, delete, or add a rule?"

4. Decide on a place to post the discussion rules where learners can refer to them at any time (poster on wall, handout, or posted on class website).

SUGGESTION

If you observe that some members of the group often violate the rules (for example, they repeatedly interrupt each other), then revisit them. Point out what you have observed, and reopen discussion of the rules and how to enforce them.

Activity 2

Discussion: Facilitating Group Discussion

PURPOSE

To promote a sense of community in which all voices are heard and respected.

METHOD

1. Ask the group to set or to read the discussion rules. Break a large group into smaller groups, if desired.

2. Prepare for the discussion by introducing a topic, defining or explaining any new vocabulary words and/or concepts, and presenting any material that must be reviewed before the discussion.

3. Present the task or goal of the discussion (e.g., Activity 4: Essential Questions or Activity 5: Defend Your Position).

4. Specify the order in which to talk, for example, clockwise around a circle.

5. Use reflective phrases to repeat learners' opinions. Emphasize relevance by referencing vocabulary or points from the reading material or discussion topic.

6. Begin by having each learner express his feelings on the topic. After all have shared, ask for additional thoughts or responses to spark discussion. Ask follow-up questions to connect learners' comments to each other or to the content. Promote in-depth discussion and critical evaluation.

7. If required, gently remind participants that they do not have to agree. Also guide the discussion so that students remain on topic.

8. When multiple people begin talking at once, specify the order in which they can share, and ask that one person speak at a time.

9. Pay attention to nonverbal communication as well as verbal; switch from discussion to other activities if learners become disengaged or the group cannot maintain discussion rules.

10. Summarize the key points of the discussion in a sentence or two at the end. If the group has broken up into small groups, have each group present a summary to the whole class.

Discussion: Building Consensus

PURPOSE

To help a group of students to discuss and come to consensus on a topic.

METHOD

1. Ask a student to read a text passage, word problem, or other stimulus for discussion. Ask students to analyze and discuss the passage in order to complete a specific task (e.g., Activity 23: Identify Main Idea and Supporting Details).

2. Divide students into pairs or small groups (3–4) and ask each individual group to come to an agreement on the assigned task (e.g., agree on and list the theme and the major supporting details).

3. Check on each pair/group and provide help if they are having trouble coming to agreement. Cultivate and encourage meaningful discussion, and make sure that all learners have a chance to speak and contribute to the task.

4. Have small groups summarize their final decisions and report them to the class. Compare answers between different groups (for example, can there be more than one right answer?) and ask groups to explain how they came to their conclusions. Ask small groups to write their answers on the board or on paper, then assign a group representative to read/explain it to the class.

SUGGESTIONS

*   Assess individual contributions either by observing the groups or by asking each learner to briefly summarize their group's decision-making process in their own words.

*   You can increase the complexity of the activity and subsequent discussion by asking small groups to do the same task (e.g., calculate the mean) with different content. Similarly, you can give all groups the same passage or problem and ask them to complete different tasks (e.g., identify the main idea, tone, or setting).

Discussion: Essential Questions

PURPOSE

To promote critical thinking by proposing questions that do not have right or wrong answers.

METHOD

1. Explain to students what essential questions are: Important questions that are broader than any one subject or even one instructional unit. They are interesting, they often spark controversy, and our answers to these questions may change over time. Essential questions can be the central focus of an instructional unit, tying together content from different subjects.

2. Prepare by selecting an essential question that could be used to analyze a text passage, set of data, or problem, but that does not have a specific right or wrong answer. You can connect the essential question to the GED test by selecting a science or social studies theme from the assessment targets (see Appendix A). An essential question generally covers more than just one assessment target.

   Sample questions:

   - How does an author's perspective impact his writing?
   - How can conflict have positive results?
   - When and how should a government protect (or limit) someone's constitutional rights?
   - Why would a person do something she knows has negative consequences?
   - What responsibility does an employer/government/corporation have toward its employees/constituents/public and vice versa?
   - How does regulation impact individual action?
   - Why would a person choose to change or not change his eating habits?

3. Before discussing the essential question, give students the text, data, or problem and time to read it silently. Read the text out loud at least once. Define vocabulary or explain as necessary to ensure comprehension.

4. Ask the essential question. If necessary, describe how it relates to the text. Ask students to answer the question.

Activity 5

Discussion: Defend Your Position

PURPOSE

To help learners read opposing views on a controversial topic, choose a position to support, and defend their choice using evidence.

METHOD

1. Select two text passages or graphics that demonstrate opposing views on a hot topic (examples: different interpretations of the First Amendment of the U.S. Constitution or two editorials representing different views on an issue).

2. Set or review discussion rules, and explain the objectives of the activity:

    a. To read/understand two different views on an issue

    b. To consider evidence used to support each position

    c. To choose a side and defend that position using evidence

3. Discuss the topic of the controversy to activate background knowledge.

4. Ask a learner to read and explain the passage for one view, and ask another learner to read and explain the other view. Ask clarifying questions, and define any new vocabulary.

5. Ask learners which position they would support. Ask all learners to choose a side. (In a small group, have each learner state his choice. In a large group, ask them to raise their hands to see who agrees with each side.) Facilitate a group discussion on the topic.

6. After learners have had a chance to talk it out, ask them to write one or two sentences about which position they chose and why.

SUGGESTION

Some controversial topics may stir up emotions or set off arguments. Remind learners that there is no right answer and all viewpoints are valid. Focus should be on citing evidence from the texts or data provided to support a position. In fact, it may be helpful for learners to choose an opinion that they do not agree with in order to practice the process with less emotional involvement.

Activity 6
Previous Lesson Review: Vocabulary

PURPOSE

To reinforce vocabulary from previous lessons.

METHOD

1. Prepare by selecting three to five vocabulary words from the previous lesson.

2. Write or display the words on a PowerPoint presentation, whiteboard, or flipchart.

3. Ask the learners to define the words.

4. Display and ask a learner to read aloud the definition of a word and an example of the word used in a sentence.

5. Remind learners to write down the words and definitions in their class notes, personal dictionaries (see Activity 10), or both.

SUGGESTION

Display clip art, graphics, or other visual cues to help students understand and remember definitions.

Activity 7
Previous Lesson Review: Spelling

PURPOSE

To practice spelling vocabulary words identified in previous activities.

METHOD

1. Prepare a list of spelling words from recent activities. Determine the length of the activity by the number of words and difficulty of definitions (for example, 5 words for a 7-minute activity or 15 words for 20 minutes). Prepare a brief definition for each word, including the part of speech.

2. Announce the spelling review and ask learners to prepare:

   a. On paper: Ask learners to get a blank piece of paper or index card.

   b. On computer: Ask learners to open the document (either a blank document or a form you have prepared).

3. Read each word aloud, and have students write the word. Leave enough time between words for all learners to finish writing.

4. After you have read every word, review the answers. Read each word again, and ask a volunteer to spell the word aloud. Ask volunteers to define each word.

5. Encourage learners to correct their own spelling, if possible. If a learner still cannot spell a word correctly, spell the word aloud for him and have him write the correct spelling.

6. Display the list of vocabulary with definitions so that learners can copy the words in their notes and/or personal dictionaries.

SUGGESTION

This can also be used at the beginning of a lesson to define terms and gauge previous knowledge of vocabulary.

Previous Lesson Review: Open Notes

PURPOSE

To reinforce previous learning and encourage independent knowledge retrieval.

METHOD

1. Prepare a list of multiple-choice questions derived from recent activities. Determine the length of the activity by the number and difficulty of questions (for example, 3 questions for a 10 minute activity or 20 questions for 45–60 minutes). Type the questions and prepare them on paper or on a computer. Create an answer key.

2. Ask learners to get out their notes from previous lessons. Explain that they will each answer a few questions to help them remember information.

3. Hand out the questions or ask learners to access questions on the computer.

4. Tell learners that they can use their notes or other in-class reference materials (no web searches) to answer all the questions.

5. When time is up, ask volunteers to give answers to questions and to explain where they found the answers.

SUGGESTIONS

- After all learners finish answering the questions independently, you can turn this into a group activity by asking them to get in pairs or small groups to discuss and compare answers. If they have different answers to a question, ask them to compare notes and come to consensus on the correct answer.

- Use as an end-of-unit activity or right before a holiday break.

- If some learners have missed classes, put them in pairs or small groups with others so they can refer to others' notes.

- Make it a game. Tell learners in advance how you will score the activity. Choose names at random to ask for the answers. If the class gets all of the questions correct, they can choose a reward.

Activity 9

Vocabulary: Preview Vocabulary

PURPOSE

To preview new vocabulary words as preparation for a lesson.

METHOD

1. Prepare a list of new vocabulary words and/or terms with definitions for the lesson. Focus on tier 2 and tier 3 words. Tier 2 words are used frequently in written material across content areas. These are words you will want your students to remember and to use. Tier 3 words are specialized and used mainly within certain content areas. Students will need to know them in order to read and write about the content. Type the list in alpha order or in the order in which terms appear in the reading.

2. Type a list of the words you identified, without definitions. Leave spaces or lines in the handout for learners to write in their own definitions. Provide spaces to add new words that are not on the list that are identified by students.

3. Go over the list of terms with learners. Ask if they recognize the words, if they can define the terms, and how they might use the words in a sentence.

4. Remind students to write down the definitions or look at their vocabulary lists for reference when defining or reviewing vocabulary in class.

SUGGESTIONS

- Provide the list of vocabulary words on a computer so that students can practice typing in definitions.

- Make a quiz using the vocabulary terms: Match definitions, match synonyms, or complete cloze sentences. Tell students you will use the scores to decide what to teach and to make sure you don't teach something they already know.

Vocabulary: Personal Dictionaries

PURPOSE

To help students organize and remember new vocabulary.

METHOD

1. Provide or suggest a place for students to keep personal dictionaries. For example a digital document, Rolodex, index cards, or notebook.

2. As students define vocabulary in class or look up new words in a dictionary, direct them to write the word, part of speech, and brief definition in their personal dictionaries. Make sure to display the word and definition with correct spelling for students to copy.

3. To enhance understanding, break longer words into parts and discuss what each part means and how the added parts—prefixes and suffixes—change the meaning of the root words. (For example, *amend* is an action word meaning to change or add, so *amendment* is the change or addition.)

4. Demonstrate or ask a student to demonstrate how to organize the vocabulary words in alphabetical order.

SUGGESTIONS:

• To aid in retention, ask students to write a sentence using the word beneath each definition.

• Suggest that students add clip art, drawings, or other visuals to definitions as appropriate.

• Collect all the vocabulary words and definitions in students' personal dictionaries during or at the end of the unit. Compile them to create a unit glossary. Make glossaries available to learners at the end of each unit for reference. Either select the definitions yourself or have students do it. Break into small groups, and assign each group several letters of the alphabet. For example, have one group compile definitions for words that start with the letters A, B, C, D, E, and F. Then assemble all the groups' definitions into one glossary.

  ▹ Add photos, clip art, or video screenshots from the unit to each vocabulary word to assist with recall.

  ▹ Use glossaries during open notes reviews.

PURPOSE

To prepare learners to use college dictionaries to define new vocabulary words.

METHOD

1. Choose five vocabulary words learners will need to know for a new unit or lesson.

2. Demonstrate how to find the first word in a dictionary you use in class. If you use an online dictionary, project the process or show screenshots.

3. Point out the different parts of the dictionary entry for the word, such as

    a. Guide words
    b. Entry word
    c. Pronunciation key
    d. Part of speech
    e. Number or letter of definitions and sub-definitions
    f. Information on word origin (etymology)

    g. Definitions
    h. Use in a sentence
    i. Variations of the word
    j. Synonyms
    k. Antonyms
    l. Picture

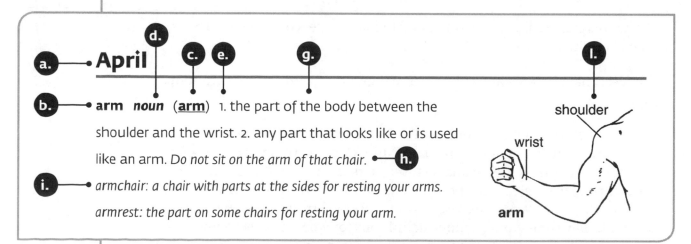

4. Create a list of labels for the parts of the entries that appear in your class dictionary. Create an answer key that shows the correct placement of labels for each of the five words.

5. Prepare the five words (collect enough dictionaries, create a handout or presentation, project from page to screen, etc) to present. Model correct placement of the labels for one of the words. Explain that "definitions" is plural because each word will likely have more than one.

6. Tell learners that you want them to practice looking up words so that they become familiar with the parts of dictionary entries and can more easily look up words on their own.

7. Have learners work alone or in pairs to find the definitions of the words and to mark (either with sticky notes or on a handout) where the labels belong. Ask them to identify which parts of the definition help them understand what the word means.

8. After learners have completed the activity, ask them if they were able to match all the labels to the entry parts. Demonstrate the correct labeling for learners.

9. Discussion questions:

   a. What do the five vocabulary words mean, as they relate to our theme?

   b. Which parts of the definition helped you understand what the words mean?

   c. Which parts of the definition did not help you understand more?

   d. What parts of the definition are you going to look for next time you look up a word in the dictionary?

SUGGESTION

Use several different dictionaries in class, and discuss the differences. Ask learners to look up the same words in different dictionaries. Ask learners to talk about what is similar and different between the parts of the dictionary entries.

Activity 12

Vocabulary: Finding the Appropriate Dictionary Definition

PURPOSE

To help learners distinguish the appropriate definition for a word from multiple definitions in the dictionary.

METHOD

1. Prepare a list of recent vocabulary words that have multiple definitions. Provide a sentence for each word that demonstrates one of the dictionary definitions.

2. Using the first word as a model, explain the objective of the activity: to practice figuring out which dictionary definition is appropriate for the context provided.

3. Demonstrate how to find the vocabulary word in the dictionary. Ask a learner to read aloud the part of speech and all the definitions (but not the origin, example sentences, etc.).

4. Ask the class which of those definitions is the most appropriate for the word as it is used in your example sentence. Talk about how to figure out which definition works. (Suggestion: Have them substitute the definition or a synonym for the word in the sentence.)

5. Ask learners to briefly rephrase the definition that they find appropriate.

6. Practice with the rest of the vocabulary words as a class, in small groups, or individually. Ask students to find the appropriate definitions for the words and to re-write the meanings in their own words. Remind learners to copy the words and appropriate definitions in their class notes or personal dictionaries.

7. Discussion questions:
   a. How did you define these words?
   b. Did you have any trouble deciding which dictionary definition to use?
   c. Did the definitions help you to understand what we've been working on?

SUGGESTIONS

- The number of vocabulary words can vary depending on your purpose and the desired length of activity.

- You could use this activity to review for a unit or to have learners fill in their personal dictionaries.

- Make this into a game by providing a long list of words and a set amount of time. See who can correctly define the most words within the time limit.

Activity 13

Vocabulary: Practice Using New Words

PURPOSE

To give learners opportunities to use and learn new words.

METHOD

1. Select a short list of vocabulary words that have all been used in recent activities.

2. Concrete examples: Present and discuss several examples of each word in use. Ask learners to take notes. After you have presented them all, ask learners to remember and write down one example for each word.

3. Sentences: Ask learners to write their own sentences using each word. Encourage them to use sentences that are funny or dramatic. This might help students remember the words.

4. Flash cards: After defining each word, ask learners to create flash cards using index cards or an online flash card creator. Another time, students can practice using flash cards in pairs or on the computer.

SUGGESTION

To make a game out of flashcard practice, provide a stopwatch or clock to each pair of learners. Use the stopwatch to determine how long it takes each person to correctly define the words on a stack of vocabulary cards. Make it clear that the game is not intended to compare students to each other, but to see how much each student can improve his time. Record the time it takes each person to correctly define all the flash cards. Occasionally return to this activity and chart improvements in students' times.

Activity 14

Vocabulary: Spot and Dot

PURPOSE

To help learners remember and use new vocabulary words by identifying them in context.

METHOD

1. Prepare by creating a list of vocabulary words that learners will encounter in a lesson. You can use this activity either right after or right before defining the vocabulary words.

2. Give learners the text passage or graphic content for the lesson in a format they can individually mark and save. Ask learners to look for and highlight the vocabulary words in the text.

3. As a whole class, ask learners where in the text or graphic they found each word.

4. Ask learners to read the words aloud as they are used in sentences.

5. Discussion prompts:

   a. Did these vocabulary words help you to figure out what this passage is about or to understand anything new about this passage?

   b. Select a vocabulary word and ask learners to use it in another sentence. Ask the class: "Was it used correctly? Does the word mean the same thing in both sentences?"

   c. Are there other places where you have heard these words used?

Vocabulary: Defining Words in Context

PURPOSE

To identify and define vocabulary words in a sentence, graphic, or passage.

METHOD

1. Prepare brief definitions for potential vocabulary words and identify parts of speech.

2. Prepare to display vocabulary words in context for students on a dry-erase board, flip chart, interactive whiteboard, or computer.

3. Introduce the passage or graphic to students. Let them scan it or read it aloud. Ask, "Are there any words you need defined?"

4. When a student asks what a word means, ask if any others know what it means. If no one knows or you need to clarify the information, give the definition yourself.

5. On your display board or computer, write the student-identified vocabulary word, its part of speech, and a brief definition.

6. As you write, show how the word breaks into sounds, syllables, roots, or prefixes/suffixes to build fluency and understanding.

7. Remind students to copy the words and definitions into their personal dictionaries.

SUGGESTIONS

• Save the identified words and definitions to use for previous lesson review or for assessment.

• Divide the list and assign a few words each to individuals, pairs, or small groups. Ask students to make an educated guess about the meaning of each word based on their previous knowledge, how it is used in the given context, and/or by using the dictionary. Have them present the meanings to the rest of the class.

• Use sentences with the vocabulary words in context to help students practice selecting the correct dictionary definition.

Activity 16

Create and Test a Hypothesis

PURPOSE

To make an educated guess and test to see if it's true.

METHOD

1. Ask learners what they think *hypothesis* means. Explain: A hypothesis is an idea that you think might be true. It is a prediction that you make based on the information you have.

2. Ask learners to predict the result or idea of the activity, process, or text you are about to address. Ask learners to write their predictions as a one-sentence hypothesis.

    a. They can predict the main idea of a text before they read it (What will this story be about?) or predict more specific information as they go along (What does this mean?).

3. Demonstrate whether the hypotheses are true by completing the activity: modeling the calculation, reading the text, watching the video, or conducting the experiment. The correct answer should become obvious so that learners will be able to see for themselves if they predicted the right answer.

SUGGESTIONS

*   Select an activity or text where some answers are clear but not self-evident from the beginning. For example, use Activity 52: Use a Punnett Square to Predict Traits. Describe the traits of parents, and have learners predict the traits of the children. They can test their hypotheses with the squares.

*   To use with small groups, ask each group to complete an activity and decide whether the hypothesis is true. Have all groups share their answers and discuss.

Activity 17

Summarize

PURPOSE

To summarize a reading passage in order to demonstrate understanding.

METHOD

1. Create a list of targeted texts, graphics, or mathematical processes connected to your theme. Select a brief passage to use as a model.

2. Present or hand out the passage to students. Have a student read aloud. Reread. Discuss to make sure that all students understand the passage.

3. Ask if students know what a summary is. If not, explain: A summary is a brief restatement that includes only the main points of a passage.

4. Model summarizing the information in one sentence. Describe how you condensed the passage down into its most important points and stated them in your own words.

5. Work together as a group to practice summarizing short passages or graphics.

6. As students become more confident summarizing, practice with longer passages. Demonstrate how you can highlight or take notes on important points as you read in order to ensure that you use them in your summary.

SUGGESTIONS

- Ask students to summarize a passage on their own. Then have them share their summaries with the class or with small groups. Have them compare their summaries and discuss the differences. Tell students not to worry about small differences in the way summaries are worded. The object is to capture the main idea in your own words, so there is no one exact answer.

- Use summarizing activities to check comprehension with new lesson content.

Activity 18

Graphic Organizer: *Sequence*

PURPOSE

To use a graphic organizer to put information in sequence.

METHOD

1. Use this sequencing activity with content you have already presented and discussed. Select a passage or problem that includes an ordered process, such as the steps of a process or calculation, a sequence of events, or the order of information on a time line or graphic.

2. Explain the objective of the activity: to put information in a sequence. Ask learners to define *sequence*: a series of things in order. Tell students that they

will use sequencing in many different ways, for instance to describe a math process, to describe events in history, or to summarize the plot of a story and recall the events in order.

3. Model the directions for the class using a simple example, such as how to test a hypothesis. First read all the steps (in random order), then ask students how to put them in the correct order. Ask which comes first, next, and last. Discuss the order of your example. Does this order make sense?

Example: Conduct an Experiment to Test a Hypothesis

1. Make observations.

2. Propose a hypothesis.

3. Design an experiment to test the hypothesis.

4. Conduct the experiment / test the hypothesis.

5. Accept or reject the hypothesis.

6. If rejected, revise hypothesis. If accepted, draw conclusions.

4. Select a passage or problem and break it into steps. Post or display the steps or parts of the process in random order. Post, display, or hand out a graphic organizer with the right number of boxes for the process.

5. Ask students to put the steps in the correct order on the graphic organizer.

6. You may want to create an answer key so that learners can check their own work when complete. Some students may finish faster than others.

7. Review the process, reread the text, or demonstrate the correct order. The correct answer should become obvious so that learners will be able to see for themselves if they put the information in the correct sequence.

SUGGESTIONS

- Provide multiple sets of information that learners have to sequence related to the same topic. Examples:

- Math: Students sequence the steps to answer a series of mixed practice problems.

- Science: First learners sequence a graphic of the process of digestion. Next learners sequence sentences describing the process of digestion.

- For longer or more complex sequences, have students work in small groups and come to a consensus on order.

Graphic Organizer: Outline

PURPOSE

To organize content using an outline format.

METHOD

1. Identify the main points and subtopics for a lesson or passage that you have recently completed. (It's easier to model this using familiar content.) Create a two- or three-level outline (1. > a. > i) with short labels or major questions from class. Create an electronic form or a handout with spaces between headings.

2. Demonstrate how to use the outline form, and ask students to fill in the outline using notes they took during the lesson.

3. Explain to students that they can also use outlines to keep track of reflections or questions while taking notes on content they learn about.

SUGGESTIONS

*   Try using the outline format with a summarizing activity for complex content. Show students how the format will help them to take notes on important points as well as to organize the points in the correct order.

    Sample outline:

---

1. Introduction

    a. What does poverty mean to you?

    b. Why is poverty important?

2. Definitions of poverty

    a. Words: definition from U.S. Census Bureau

    b. Experience: "Rural Poverty in the United States" YouTube video from World Vision

    c. The Numbers: Health and Human Services Poverty Guidelines

3. What can we do about it?

    a. "Education Pays" graph from Bureau of Labor Statistics

---

                    i.

                    ii.

             b. What predicts a child's achievement?

                    i.

                    ii.

             c. What can I do about poverty?

                    i.

                    ii.

                    iii.

Graphic Organizer: Venn Diagram

PURPOSE

To use a Venn diagram to compare and contrast two or more things.

METHOD

1. Decide on content for demonstrating the use of a Venn diagram. (Choose two things to compare and contrast.) Create a blank diagram on the board or on a computer display.

2. Present the content and have learners read it. Explain that the content describes two things that are similar in some ways and different in some ways. A Venn diagram is a way to visualize the differences and similarities. Some possible examples:

    a. Traits of two or three main characters in a fictional passage.

    b. Major responsibilities of federal and state governments.

    c. Qualities of various energy resources: solar, coal, and nuclear (pollution, cost, availability, etc.).

    d. Key features of two graphs or data displays (intercepts, maximums and minimums, symmetries).

3. Ask learners what the concepts have in common. Write this information in the overlapping portion of the diagram.

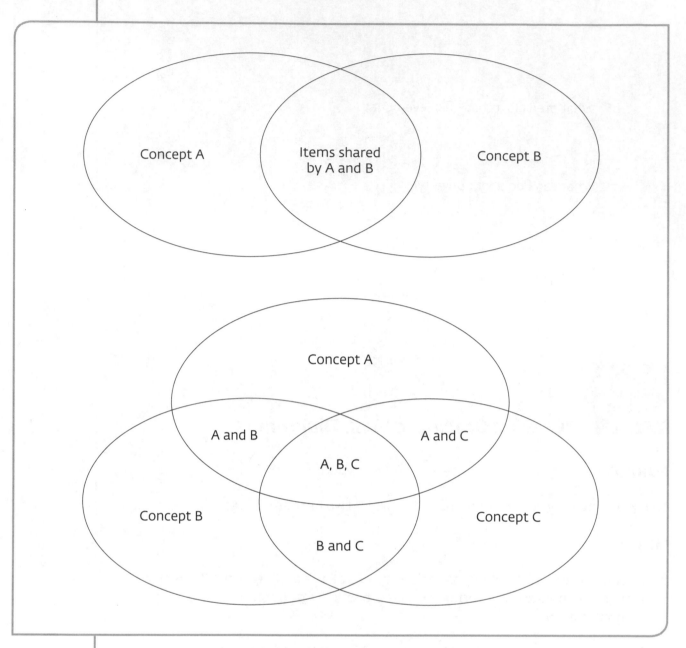

4. Ask learners what is different about the concepts. Write this information in the appropriate portions of the circles.

5. Review the completed diagram and solicit any additional questions. Discuss how the diagram shows a summary of key similarities and differences between the two concepts.

SUGGESTIONS

• Learners can write characteristics on sticky notes and attach to a board with the diagram.

• Venn diagrams can also be used to brainstorm or organize information for writing. Consider using this when working on writing comparison/contrast essays.

Graphic Organizer: Pros and Cons

PURPOSE

To use a graphic organizer to evaluate the pros and cons of an idea.

METHOD

1. Identify one or two passages or sets of data that describes a position for or against a decision related to your theme. Examples:

   a. Social Studies: Should the U.S. get involved in World War I? Would you have voted for or against the War in Iraq in 2003?

   b. Science: Energy. Should the city install wind turbines to produce energy?

   c. Math: Finances. Should a workers' union offer retirement plans?

2. Describe the sample scenario and the purpose for the activity: to visualize and weigh the arguments for and against a decision.

3. Create or ask learners to create a T-chart with a name for the decision on the top and a line down the middle of the page. Label one column "Pros" and the other "Cons." Explain that pros are arguments or reasons in favor of something and cons are arguments against something.

Should the U.S. get involved in World War I?	
PROS	**CONS**

4. Ask learners to name some reasons for or against the decision. Write the ideas in the correct columns.

Should the U.S. get involved in World War I?	
PROS	**CONS**
Germany is sinking U.S. submarines. More U.S. citizens could be drafted into the military. It might increase trade with other countries.	The U.S. has not been involved in European affairs since the Revolutionary War. Immigrants came to the U.S. to get away from war and poverty in Europe. Europe is across the ocean.

5. After generating a list of ideas, ask a learner to re-read what has been written. Ask if anyone wants to make any changes or can combine any items.

6. Initiate a discussion of the reasons for or against the decision.

7. Ask learners to vote on what decision they would make in the scenario. Did the pros and cons help them to make their decision?

SUGGESTIONS

• Extend this activity by asking learners to choose a position based on the evidence presented. You can follow this with activities like "Defend a Position" or ask learners to write a short-answer response.

• Talk about ways that learners might use pros and cons to make decisions in their personal lives. Ask them for examples of situations where this might be useful, such as deciding on where to go for vacation, deciding on what to buy someone for a gift, deciding on what class to take, etc.

The Reasoning through Language Arts Test

Overview

The Reasoning through Language Arts (RLA) Test integrates reading, writing, and language assessment targets. The focus is on demonstrating skills in three domains:

1. Reading: Read, comprehend, and analyze complex text

2. Writing: Write a well-developed argument using supporting evidence

3. Language: Edit text in context to eliminate errors and nonstandard usage

The RLA Test is 150 minutes long, with one ten-minute break. There are approximately 51 questions. Multiple-choice items are worth 1 point each, but other item types may be worth 1, 2, or 3 points. The extended response is worth 12 points, the balance of the test is worth 53 points, and the total test has a maximum point score of 65.

The extended response item appears somewhere in the middle of the test—it is not the first or last item. Instead, the test begins with a variety of item types. After a test-taker completes those items, the extended response activity begins. Once the extended response item begins, the test-taker has 45 minutes to type a response and will not be able to return to the first part of the test. Any extra time left after the first part of the test is not added to any other part of the test. When the extended response is submitted, the ten-minute break begins. At the end of the break, the second half of the RLA Test launches, so test-takers will lose time if they do not return promptly from the break.

Item Types

More than half of the test items will be traditional multiple choice questions with four answer options. In addition, the test will include the following interactive item types:

- Drag-and-drop: Move an image, word, or phrase to the correct position within a graphic organizer or move sentences to reorder them within a paragraph

- Drop-down: Choose the correct answer (word, phrase, or sentence) from menu options embedded within a passage

- Fill-in-the-blank: Type a word, phrase, or sentence to answer a question or complete a passage

- Extended response: Type a well-developed, supported response to a prompt based on two passages, citing evidence from the passages and using standard English conventions

Approximately 80 percent of the items will involve a cognitive complexity or DOK level of two or three. The rest of the items will be at level one.

Content

Reading Assessment

Reading comprehension passage sets will range from 400 to 900 words and include six to eight test items. Reading passages will cover a range of complexity, including some at the career- and college-readiness levels. Seventy-five percent of the text passages on the RLA Test will be informational or nonfiction texts drawn from science and social studies content as well as a variety of workplace contexts. Twenty-five percent of passages will be literature. Text passages will vary in level, up to and including career- and college-readiness levels.

The reading comprehension targets are guided by the main objectives of CCSS Anchor Standards 1 and 10 for reading:

- Read closely to determine the details of what the text explicitly states and make logical inferences or valid claims supported by textual evidence.

- Read and respond to questions on a range of complex literary and informational texts.

Assessment targets and indicators are also derived from the CCSS and include these skills:

- Determining main idea and supporting details

- Analyzing how characters and events develop and interact

- Interpreting language and understanding word choice

- Analyzing the structure and how parts of a text relate to each other and the whole

- Determining the author's purpose or point of view

- Evaluating the author's argument or claims and assessing the validity of the evidence

- Comparing two or more texts, synthesizing the information, and analyzing the differences

Writing Assessment

Reading and writing are integrated on the new test, as evidenced by the extended response item. Test-takers will analyze two text passages totaling up to 650 words that describe opposing views on a topic. A prompt will require them to write a well developed and supported argument based on the passages. Test-takers will be able to use an erasable noteboard to plan their essays. Basic word processing tools will be available when they type their essays into the computer: cut, copy, paste, undo, and redo. Standard keyboard shortcuts for these tools will also work.

The writing targets reflect the main objectives of CCSS Anchor Standards 9 and 6 for writing:

- Draw relevant and sufficient evidence from literary or informational text to support analysis and reflection.

- Use technology and a sufficient command of keyboarding skills to produce writing.

Extended responses will be scored by computer according to these three traits:

1. Creation of argument and use of evidence

2. Development of ideas and organizational structure

3. Clarity and command of standard English conventions

Each trait is scored from 0 to 2 points. The score is double-weighted for a total raw score of 12 possible points. Unless a response is flagged by the computer as requiring human scoring, the score will be delivered within three hours. The complete scoring rubric is shown in Appendix B.

The stimulus passages and item prompt will appear on a split screen. Test-takers can refer to the passage on the left while they type into the box on the right. They will not be able to copy and paste text from the passage into their responses. Though there is no minimum or maximum length set for the response, a thorough response is expected to include several paragraphs.

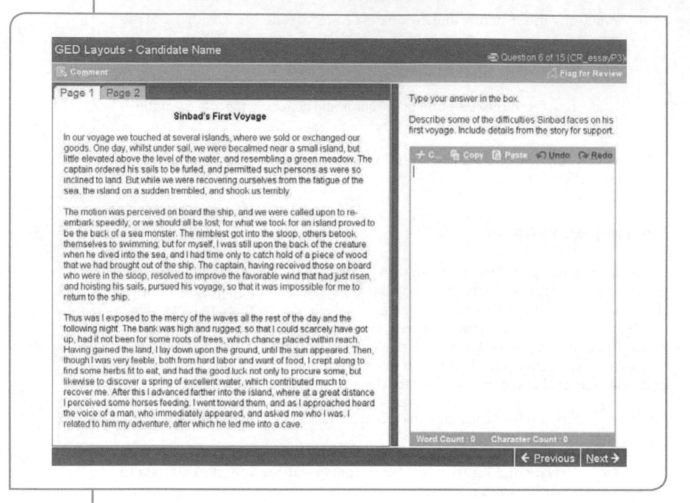

Language Assessment

The language skills items on the test are presented in a new way. Drop-down menu boxes within a text passage give test-takers a menu choice of four options. Embedding the options within passages allows test-takers to read and evaluate the answer in context. When an answer is selected, it will appear on the screen as part of the text. Each item will require a response in order for the sentence or paragraph to be complete.

Language targets are derived from a set of foundational skills identified by college instructors as being necessary for success in entry-level college composition courses. These skills include essential components of grammar, usage, capitalization, and punctuation.

The complete reading, writing, and language assessment targets and indicators are listed in Appendix A.

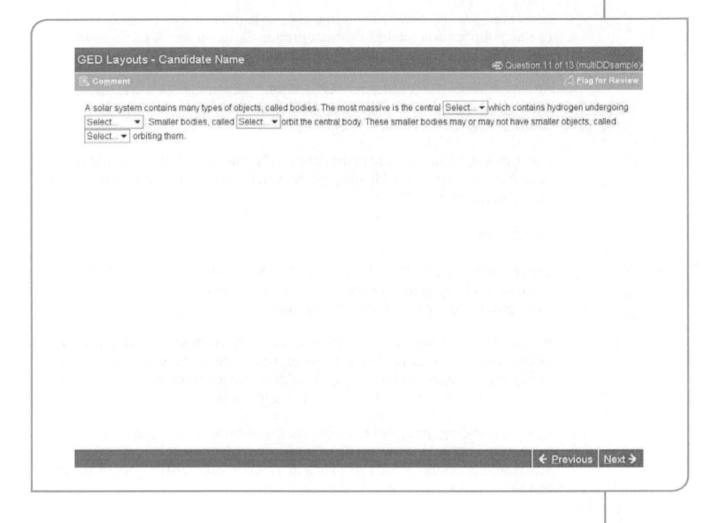

Comment   Flag for Review

A solar system contains many types of objects, called bodies. The most massive is the central [Select... ▼] which contains hydrogen undergoing [Select... ▼]. Smaller bodies, called [Select... ▼] orbit the central body. These smaller bodies may or may not have smaller objects, called [Select... ▼] orbiting them.

← Previous   Next →

Activity 22

Read It Twice

PURPOSE

To increase reading fluency through reading aloud and listening to texts.

METHOD

1. Select and prepare text passage(s) as handouts or to project or present electronically.

2. Introduce the reading topic, and preview any necessary vocabulary words/ terms.

3. Ask learners to read the text silently. Tell them you will be asking them to read aloud afterward.

4. After everyone has finished reading, ask one learner to read the text aloud to the group. Gently model or correct pronunciation of words critical for comprehension of the passage, if necessary.

5. After one person has read aloud, ask a second person to read the text aloud again. Explain that the purpose is to hear a second voice. Ask learners to listen carefully and follow along in their text.

6. Ask learners, "What did you learn listening to the reading that you did not remember when you read it silently? Did you learn anything new the second time you heard it read?"

SUGGESTIONS

- Use this reading activity to have learners practice summarizing or finding the main idea. After reading a short text twice, ask them to either summarize it in their own words or to describe the main idea.

- Prepare two or three texts and either assign different texts to different learners or give learners a choice of which text to read. Instead of reading to the whole group, put learners in pairs or groups of three with others who have a different text. Have them read aloud to each other and discuss.

- Use with reading prompts or complex test questions to reinforce the importance of understanding what is being asked before learners respond. Stress that learners should reread (silently) every test question, especially fill-in-the blank and constructed response items.

Activity
23
Identify Main Idea and Supporting Details

PURPOSE

To help learners identify the main idea and key supporting details in a complex text.

METHOD

1. Select a text passage (400–900 words long).

2. If learners are not familiar with main or central idea and supporting details, explain or review. Use a short sample text to model finding them before moving on to the longer passage.

3. Prepare texts in a format for learners to circle, highlight, or underline content. You may want to make sure they have highlighters or colored pens. You may demonstrate how to highlight text on a computer if students are reading on the screen.

4. Explain that the objective is to identify the central or main idea and major supporting details.

5. Introduce the text passage that you will be reading. Read the title (and author, if there is one). Discuss the topic. Ask, "Based on the title, what do you think this passage will be about?"

6. Ask learners to first read the text silently. After most or all students have finished reading silently, ask for volunteers to read it aloud.

7. Ask learners to underline, circle, or highlight one phrase or sentence in the text that states the main idea. Give them time to find it on their own.

8. After learners complete the task individually, ask the whole class, "What was the main idea? Where was it stated in the text?" Discuss how they found it. "What clues led you to the main idea?" Learners may choose different sentences. Explain that the main idea may be stated more than once and in more than one way. If some learners had trouble finding the main idea on their own or were unsure, point out some tips for identifying main idea:

   a. Reread: Reread the title and the first sentence. Read the last sentence.

   b. Repeat: Look for an idea that is repeated several times.

   c. Restate: Try to summarize the passage. What is the key point in your own words?

   d. Reinforce: If you are not sure an idea is the main idea, look at the details. Are there facts or examples that support it?

9. Ask learners to define a supporting detail: an example, story, or argument that supports the main idea. Give examples using a brief sample text if necessary.

10. Ask learners to re-read the same text and mark the supporting details. After they complete the task individually, ask learners to talk about the supporting points they identified.

11. Discuss:

   a. Which are the strongest, most important details that support the main idea?

   b. How were the supporting points organized (time order, definition, order of importance, by categories, cause and effect, compare and contrast)?

   c. Where did you find the supporting details in relation to the main idea?

12. Extension discussion: "What did you learn about main idea and details that you can use in your own writing?" Sample learning points:

a. Clearly state your main idea.

b. The organization of supporting details depends on what they are and how they relate to the main idea.

c. Connect all details to the main idea. If a detail is not directly related to the main idea, don't use it.

SUGGESTIONS

- If the main idea of a passage is unstated or implied, reverse the order and look for details first. Initiate discussion of the details and have learners guess or infer the main idea.

- Select two or three texts for the activity. Use the additional texts for homework or in-class practice.

- If your learners write essays, have them practice finding the main idea and details of each other's writing. This can spin off into a writing/revising activity: Have learners work in pairs and offer each other feedback on how to clarify their main points.

Activity
24

Graphic Organizer: Main Idea Map

PURPOSE

To help learners understand main idea and supporting details by using a graphic organizer.

METHOD

1. Hand out or demonstrate how to draw a graphic organizer with a space at the top, labeled "Main Idea" and blank space underneath.

2. Show learners how to complete the organizer by adding details below the main idea.

3. Ask learners to read a text and identify the main idea. Have them write the main idea on the top of their organizers.

4. Ask learners to look for details that support the main idea. Have them write each detail below the main idea and connect the ideas with lines.

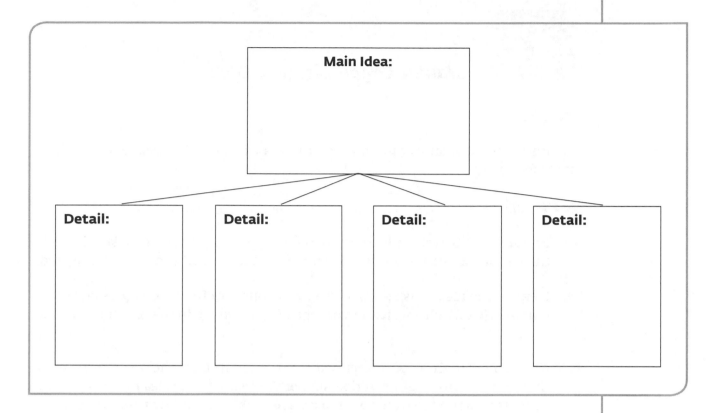

Main Idea:

Detail:

Detail:

Detail:

Detail:

SUGGESTIONS

- Have learners use the graphic organizer when analyzing an argument. Have them read the argument, and fill in the organizer. Then ask them to look at the main argument and the points that support it. Ask them if the supporting details are strong enough to convince them that the argument is true.

- Use this graphic organizer to brainstorm ideas for writing an essay (such as the extended response). Tell learners that it not only helps them to organize their ideas, but that looking at ideas in this format helps them to see if their details are strong enough to support their main idea.

- Learners can also use this activity to reflect on their own writing or to evaluate each other's writing.

Graphic Organizer: Idea Web

PURPOSE

To use a graphic organizer to connect ideas as a way to analyze text or organize ideas for writing.

METHOD

1. Prepare a blank web for learners to use or demonstrate how to make one. Tell them that they can use a web to demonstrate how details in a text are related.

2. Identify one idea or ask learners to suggest one idea from a text passage. Write that idea (word, phrase, name, concept, etc.) in a circle in the center of a blank page.

3. Ask learners to think of at least two or three details from the text that relate to that idea. Details might describe, support, or relate to the idea in any way. Ask learners to write the words or phrases in circles surrounding the main circle, with lines connecting them to the main circle.

4. Ask learners if they can find any details in the text that relate to or help to describe an idea in one of the detail circles. Demonstrate how to branch off one of the detail circles to show details that relate to it.

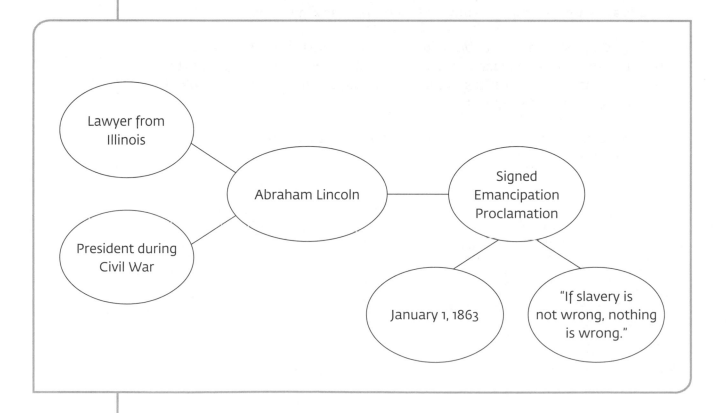

SUGGESTIONS

- To use with a prepared text, you may want to identify the idea to be the center of your web. Create a key with a list of appropriate answers for the supporting details or traits.

- Have learners work on their own to make webs for a reading passage. Then have them work in pairs or small groups to compare their webs. Talk about the differences in the way they drew their webs and the ideas they chose to connect. Ask, "Why don't all the webs look the same?"

- Have learners use webs to brainstorm before a writing activity. Tell them to start with the main idea of their writing and then branch off to supporting points. Then they can connect details about their supporting points.

Make a Supported Argument

PURPOSE

To practice presenting an argument and citing evidence to support it.

METHOD

1. First, use a short sample text (like a brief newspaper article) to demonstrate how to find the author's main point or argument and some important details that support it. Restate the argument and details, in your own words, in a convincing way. Ask learners if they believe that your point is valid.

2. Have learners work in pairs or small groups. Give each group a different article or passage. Learners can mark up (circle or highlight) the main argument and supporting details in their articles.

3. Explain the objective: to practice presenting a main idea and citing evidence from the text to support it. Tell them to use at least one direct quote from the article when making their case.

4. Ask the groups to write down, in their own words:

   a. The main point of their argument

   b. At least two or three details in support of their argument

   c. At least one direct quote from the article that supports their argument

5. Have each group present their argument to the class.

6. You may ask clarifying questions, if necessary. After each argument has been presented, ask the class if the argument is logical and the group has made its case.

7. If the class agrees that an argument is not fully supported, discuss what could be changed to make a better supported argument.

SUGGESTION

Use after Activity 5: Defend Your Position, and assign groups based on their selections.

Identify the Theme

PURPOSE

To help learners identify a theme that connects multiple texts.

METHOD

1. Ask if learners know what the word *theme* means. Answer: It's a central idea or topic of a text or graphic. It may also be the moral or meaning of a work of fiction. There may be more than one theme, and a theme may or may not be the main idea.

2. To make sure learners understand theme, present three short texts and/or graphics, such as articles, cartoons, or short stories that share one common theme. Ask the group:

   a. What one idea or topic do all three works have in common?

   b. How do you know? What details do you see in each work that point to that theme?

   c. Is the theme of each also the main idea?

3. To connect the idea of theme to a current unit, prepare two short texts (200–500 words) related to your unit theme.

4. Give each learner one of the readings. Either use handouts so that they can mark them up and write in the margins, use sticky notes to mark up readings in a book, or have learners take notes on paper.

5. Ask learners to talk about the titles and authors of their readings. Ask what they think the text will be about.

6. Have learners read silently. After reading, ask them to write at least one theme they identify in the reading. Ask them to underline or note details about the theme.

7. After learners have finished reading and marking up the texts, put them in small groups with others who have read the same texts. Ask them to share with the group the themes they identified and the details. Have groups discuss similarities and differences and take notes on what they find.

8. Ask for volunteers to read each of the texts aloud to the whole group.

9. Have learners from the small groups share what they identified as the theme(s). Discuss:

    a. Is there one theme that connects the two readings? What do they have in common?

    b. Did you identify more than one theme in each of the readings?

    c. Can you connect any other recent readings to one of these themes?

    d. How did you identify the theme? How was the theme presented in the readings?

SUGGESTIONS

- For multilevel classrooms, you can use texts written at different levels that share a theme.

- You can also use this activity with complex technical or historical texts. Preview new vocabulary before reading. Have learners read the texts once, and then discuss the common themes. After rereading and discussing to enhance comprehension, ask if learners can identify any more connections between the readings.

- Use this as a warm-up activity for interdisciplinary lessons or activities.

Activity
28

Fill in the Blanks with Descriptive Words

PURPOSE

To help learners identify and understand the relevance of detailed descriptions of characters, ideas, or events and how they relate to the overall meaning or theme of a text passage.

METHOD

1. Prepare a short text passage (200 words or less) that includes adjectives and adverbs to describe key elements (characters, organizations, ideas, places, historical events, theme, etc.) of the text. Identify the descriptive words.

2. Create a list of the adjectives and adverbs from the text, along with an equal number of incorrect descriptive words.

3. Create a cloze or fill-in-the-blank version of the text, substituting blanks for descriptive words.

4. First ask learners to read the complete text silently or aloud. Help with vocabulary, as necessary, and make sure learners understand the basic meaning of the text.

5. Replace the complete text with the fill-in-the-blank version. Also present the list of descriptive words to learners.

6. Demonstrate how to select one of the adjectives or adverbs from the list to fill in a blank. Discuss how the descriptive word changes the meaning of the sentence. Write in an incorrect word, and ask if learners can tell that the word does not belong. (It changes the meaning of the sentence, incorrectly describes the character or place, etc.)

7. Ask learners either individually or in pairs to fill in the rest of the blanks in the text using words from the list. Allow learners to use dictionaries, vocabulary lists, and other reference tools to complete the activity.

8. As a large group, review the words selected for each blank. Ask learners who selected the correct answer to explain why or how they chose that word.

9. After reviewing the answers, ask a learner to read the complete text aloud. Discuss how the descriptive words change or enhance the meaning of the text.

SUGGESTIONS

- Extend the activity by discussing the particular descriptive words that were used in the text and how they may relate to each other. Do the descriptions have anything in common? Compare types of descriptions to each other—for instance, sort character trait descriptions by character and compare the lists to find out what they say about the characters, or sort adverbs and discuss how the descriptions of actions in the passage contribute to the overall mood or tone.

- Use this activity to focus on one particular type of descriptive words, such as character traits. Use a text passage with multiple characters, and have learners fill in the appropriate traits for each character. Compare characters by making a traits web for each (see Activity 29).

- You can continue to work with the text by using other reading activities after this exercise.

- This activity can also be used as a review or quiz, either on paper or on computer.

TEACHING ADULTS: A GED® TEST RESOURCE BOOK

Graphic Organizer: Traits Web

PURPOSE

To help learners identify and analyze character traits using a graphic organizer.

METHOD

1. Select a medium length text (200–450 words) related to your theme.

2. Identify two or more central characters.

3. For each character, create a list of three correct traits and three incorrect traits.

4. With learners, read the text, define vocabulary, discuss content, etc.

5. Ask learners to create or fill in a web graphic organizer with one center circle and three connected circles.

6. Model using the web by having learners write the name of a central character in the center circle. Show them the list of six traits, and ask learners which three they should write in the web. Discuss their answers, and make sure they understand which answers are correct.

7. Give the learners the name of a second character and a list of six traits. Ask learners to fill out trait webs independently.

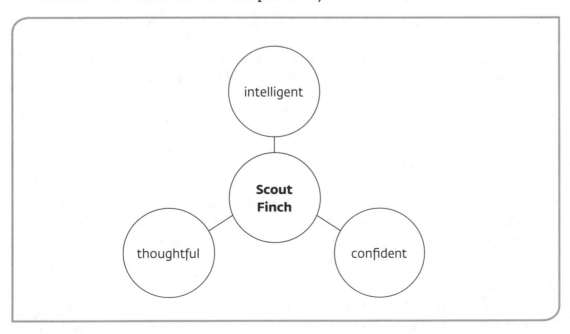

SUGGESTION

If desired, prepare a paper or digital graphic organizer for learners to complete.

Activity 30

Discussion: Understanding Complex Texts

PURPOSE

To introduce a discussion process that students can use to increase their comprehension of complex texts.

METHOD

1. Prepare by selecting a complex or dense text passage. Length can vary from one paragraph with high historic, scientific, or literary significance to passages up to 650 words. A complex text is one that requires readers to make inferences for comprehension or to define new vocabulary or technical vocabulary that is specific to the context. It may also be set in an unfamiliar context, such as a historic time. Here are some questions to help you determine whether a text is dense:

    a. Is the vocabulary especially difficult? Does it include words or phrases that are used mainly in specific disciplines? Is the vocabulary figurative rather than literal? Does it require background knowledge in another language or culture?

    b. Is the reading level, text complexity, or Lexile level higher than what students are used to? Are the sentences especially long or complicated?

    c. How much work do readers have to do to comprehend the text? Is the meaning implicit or are there multiple levels of meaning?

    d. Does the text have a complex or unconventional structure?

2. Select a task for students to complete, such as making and verifying a prediction, identifying the author's purpose, or finding the main idea.

3. Before introducing the text, preview the topic and text to familiarize students with the context. (For instance, if you are discussing Hamlet's soliloquy, first describe the character and the setting, and make sure students understand the plot of the play so far.)

4. Explain to the class that they will be given a specific task to complete using the text after they read and understand it. (For instance, have students read only the first line and then predict what Hamlet talks about in the soliloquy.)

5. Present the text, and read the entire text aloud once.

6. Ask students to point out words that need to be defined. After you help students define and understand the vocabulary, have a student reread the passage aloud.

7. Ask students what questions they have about the text. Discuss.

8. After sufficient comprehension discussion, describe the task and ask students to complete it either individually or in small groups. You may want to use the Building Consensus activity as a guideline for group discussions.

9. After groups have agreed on their responses to the task, have them report to the whole group. (Were your predictions correct? What was Hamlet talking/ thinking about?) Compare answers, and discuss as a group.

SUGGESTIONS

- You can check general class comprehension with a set of review questions before assigning the task. You can also use review questions to assess individual comprehension. Consider grouping students according to their comprehension level or mixing groups so that students with better comprehension can help others.

- Introduce a dense text at least once per unit. You can also re-introduce the same dense text at different times, for different purposes. Narrowing the task on hand, and revisiting the text multiple times may increase depth of comprehension.

- Be sure to introduce controversial or emotional topics ahead of time. Allow students to talk to you privately if certain topics (such as suicide) will be difficult for them. Sound policies can help you plan ahead to give students options such as not participating in group discussion on a sensitive topic.

Activity
31
Focused Freewriting

PURPOSE

To develop a process for learners to communicate effectively, through responses by focusing on content.

METHOD

1. Select a brief text passage or graphic and develop a sample constructed response question related to it.

2. Tell learners that they will read a passage and a prompt about the passage. Then they will write a response to the prompt.

3. Prepare learners to work either on paper or on the computer.

4. Give learners the following directions:
   a. First read the passage and the prompt.

b. Next, write or type for five or ten minutes about the topic, depending on complexity.

c. Tell them not to worry about spelling, grammar, or punctuation. They will not be graded.

d. Tell them to focus on recording their ideas about the topic.

5. Have learners discuss their ideas either in pairs or as a group. Does their writing answer the question fully? Is it a good first draft? What would they do next if they had to submit a complete response?

SUGGESTION

Repeat this activity with different texts, graphics, and questions until learners are comfortable writing or typing their ideas. Ask them to select one of their focused free-writings to expand into an extended response (see Activity 33).

Activity 32

Unpacking a Prompt

PURPOSE

To help students analyze writing prompts.

METHOD

1. Find or write a prompt for an extended response question to use for class practice. You will also need a sample prompt to use as an example. You can use the prompts in the RLA and Social Studies Item Samplers, if you'd like.

2. Explain to students that the extended response prompts for RLA and Social Studies will be similar in two ways: They will both require students to read and analyze passages. And they will both require students to write a supported argument or position related to the passages. Show students one of the prompts with its passage(s).

3. First read the passage(s). Tell students that they should read the source passages first so that they have the context they need to understand the prompt. Let students read the passage silently. Answer any questions, or discuss briefly to ensure students comprehend the material.

4. Ask students to read the prompt silently. Then ask a student to read the prompt aloud. Ask students to identify the three parts of the prompt:

    a. Part 1: a summary or statement about the content in the passage(s).

    b. Part 2: a description of what to do and what your writing should include.

c. Part 3: instructions for completing the task.

Sample prompt from RLA Item Sampler:

> While Dr. Silverton's speech outlines the benefits of cloud seeding, the editorial identifies drawbacks of this process. } Part 1
>
> In your response, analyze both the speech and the editorial to determine which position is best supported. Use relevant and specific evidence from both sources to support your response. } Part 2
>
> Type your response in the box. This task may require approximately 45 minutes to complete. } Part 3

5. Talk about the first part of the prompt. Ask students if they recognize the ideas that are mentioned. Ask students, "Do you remember some of the benefits of cloud seeding? Do you remember some of the drawbacks?" Explain that understanding the ideas pointed out in Part 1 is key to understanding and responding to the prompt. You may want to extend this discussion by using Activity 21: Pros and Cons. Write "Cloud Seeding" at the top of the T-chart. Ask students to name pros and cons from the two passages, and write them in the appropriate column.

6. Have students read Part 2 of the prompt again. Explain that this part of the prompt tells them exactly what they need to do and what they must include in their answer. Ask students to answer these questions in their own words, "What is the first thing you must do?" (read and understand the speech and the editorial) "What is the second thing you must do?" (decide which is the stronger argument, the speech or the editorial) "What must your response include?" (details from both viewpoints that back up my position)

7. Review Part 3 of the prompt. Explain that the extended responses will be timed separately from the rest of the test. Students will be able to see (or hide) a clock that counts down the time they have to write. They have 45 minutes for the RLA response and 25 minutes for Social Studies.

8. Tell students that they will have a erasable noteboard to write on during the test. They can use it to take notes or to outline their responses. You may want to continue with Activity 34: Four Steps to Writing an Extended Response.

Activity 33

Introducing Extended Response Scoring

PURPOSE

To familiarize students with the scoring process for RLA extended responses.

METHOD

1. Find a well-written extended response essay to use as an example. (Create your own, or see the sample response in the RLA Item Sampler at www.gedtestingservice.com.) Make sure that you have the stimulus passage(s) and prompt. The essay should cite evidence and score well on the RLA extended response rubric. Choose a score with an explanation according to the writing rubric.

2. Provide students with a copy of the essay, stimulus, and prompt. Hand out or project the scoring rubric for students to see.

3. First read and discuss each item in the rubric. If students are not familiar with rubrics, explain how a score is determined for each of the three traits. You may want to discuss the traits one at a time, to focus on helping students understand the requirements. If students have used rubrics before, you may be able to just review the details of each trait and determine an overall score. Define terms and discuss examples in order to ensure students understand the rubric.

4. Ask students to silently read the stimulus, prompt, and example response. Then ask for volunteers to read them aloud.

5. Either as a class or in small groups, have students evaluate and score the essay. Start with Trait 1, and have them review the requirements for a score of 4. Ask, "Does this essay deserve a 4?" If all students do not agree, then review the requirements for a score of 3. Ask if the essay should get 3 points, etc. Have groups total their scores for the essay, or agree on a score as a class.

6. Discuss how students scored the responses. If anyone scored the essay too high or too low, refer back to the scoring rubric and discuss.

SUGGESTIONS

- Ask students to write an extended response on the same topic, or give them a different prompt that refers to the same stimulus. Have students grade their own or each other's essays using the rubric.

- As students practice writing extended responses, have them refer to the rubric and rewrite essays that score poorly the first time.

Four Steps to Writing an Extended Response

PURPOSE

To use a four-step process to write a multi-paragraph, supported response with a well-developed thesis.

METHOD

1. Select one or two longer texts (450–900 words total) written at the 8–10 grade level that are related to your theme. The text(s) should demonstrate two different points of view on an issue.

2. Write a prompt that will require students to analyze the text, state a position, and support it with evidence.

3. Introduce the activity. Students who are not comfortable using a computer can practice writing responses on paper. After they have practiced the process of writing a supported argument, then they can move to the computer. Students with good keyboarding skills may want to practice on the computer right away. Review the steps for writing good responses and make sure students have extra paper or graphic organizer templates to use for planning. Tell students that they will have a erasable noteboard to use for planning their responses on the GED test.

   • Step 1 Read: Read the passage(s) and unpack the prompt.

   • Step 2 Plan: Make notes, organize your ideas, and plan your writing.

   • Step 3 Write: Write your ideas using your plan to guide you. Be sure to cite specific details from the passage to support your position.

   • Step 4 Review and Edit: Read your response and check that you have thoroughly answered the question. Make sure you have clearly stated your thesis and supported it with examples. Then check grammar, usage, and spelling.

4. Explain the objectives of the activity:

   • Read about two perspectives on an issue, and write a clearly stated thesis that supports one perspective.

   • Develop an argument that supports the thesis by citing relevant information from the text.

   • Organize your writing into paragraphs that show a logical progression of ideas.

   • Edit and revise writing to ensure proper spelling and grammar.

5. Provide the prompt and ask students to read it silently. You may want to use Activity 32: Unpacking a Prompt to get started and make sure students understand the task.

6. Remind students how to create (or where to find) graphic organizers to use for brainstorming. You may want to demonstrate using a T-chart like the one in Activity 21: Pros and Cons. Show students how they can use a chart to take notes on the evidence they will cite. In this way, they can make a plan: Write about one detail in each paragraph, write about the details in a specific order, and keep track of which details they have included as they type.

7. Have students write their responses, either in class or as homework. Keep track of the time, or have them keep track of their own time. Tell them it's okay to take longer than the 25 or 45 minutes this time, but that with practice they should improve their time.

8. Score responses according to the extended response writing scoring rubric. Provide score and feedback individually as soon as possible.

SUGGESTIONS

- After you are sure that students understand the process and have had practice writing extended responses, have them take timed tests. Simulate the GED test experience by having students type their responses directly onto a blank document using word processing software. Allow 45 minutes for the RLA extended response or 25 minutes for the social studies extended response. At first, you may want to tell them that the time is up and allow them to finish. With practice, students should be able to complete their responses within the time allowed.

- Many students will feel more comfortable writing first on paper and then typing up their responses. This is fine as an intermediate step for those who need practice with computer skills or keyboarding. But they should get plenty of practice typing responses in order to feel comfortable when they take the test.

- To use this activity to practice social studies extended responses, be sure to tell students that they will only have 25 minutes.

- This is a good end-of-unit writing activity. After students have a good understanding of a topic and have had the chance to talk about it and ask questions, then you could introduce a writing prompt. Allow them to refer to their books or notes to find details or quotes to support their writing. Students can grade their own or each other's writing using the scoring rubric.

Activity
35

Editing to Correct Grammatical Errors

PURPOSE

To help the learners develop a process for editing to correct grammatical or mechanical errors.

METHOD

1. Prepare an unedited writing draft to use as a model.

2. Review and discuss with learners the items in Trait 3 of the RLA scoring rubric:

    Trait 3: Clarity and Command of Standard English Conventions (maximum 4 points)

    Conventions

    ▷ Frequently confused words, homonyms, and contractions: passed, past; two, to, too; there, their, they're; knew, new; it's, its

    ▷ Subject-verb agreement

    ▷ Pronoun usage: antecedent agreement, unclear references, case

    ▷ Placement of modifiers and correct word order

    ▷ Capitalization: proper nouns, titles, and beginnings of sentences

    ▷ Use of apostrophes with possessive nouns

    ▷ Use of punctuation: serial commas, end marks, clause separation

    Sentence structure and fluency

    ▷ Correct subordination, coordination, and parallelism

    ▷ Avoidance of wordiness and awkward sentence structure

    ▷ Use of transitional words, conjunctive adverbs, and other words that support logical progression and clarity

    ▷ Avoidance of run-on sentences, fused sentences, or sentence fragments

    ▷ Standard usage at a level of formality appropriate for on-demand, draft writing

    Contains few or no errors in mechanics and conventions

3. Model reading the draft to look for errors. Read the first sentence (with an error). Point out the error, and correct it. Then, ask learners to read the next sentence(s) silently, and raise their hands when they spot an error. After several learners have raised their hands, ask them:

    a. What error did you find? (Is it on the list of conventions in the rubric?)

    b. How would you correct the error?

4. If necessary, discuss the grammar or mechanics rule that relates to the error. Make sure learners understand what was wrong, why it was wrong, and how to correct it.

5. Have learners continue reading silently and mark (underline or highlight) errors that they find. When everyone has finished, go through the errors one at a time. If a learner points out an error but the sentence is correct, ask the other students if they agree. If possible, have another student explain why the sentence is correct as it is. Continue to go through the writing, with learners pointing out errors. Discuss and, if necessary, model how to correct the mistakes.

6. When you have finished going through the draft, review the list of conventions in Trait 3 of the rubric. Ask learners if they are satisfied that the writing deserves the maximum score. Do they see anything else that needs to be corrected?

7. Ask learners to rewrite the draft, correcting all of the errors in their own words. Have them work in pairs to score the drafts using Trait 3 of the rubric.

SUGGESTION

Have learners select a previous essay that they think they can improve. Ask them to first underline or highlight any errors. Then have them rewrite the essay, correcting the errors.

Activity 36

Using an Editing Checklist

PURPOSE

To offer learners a checklist to use to practice editing.

METHOD

1. Introduce the editing checklist to learners. Review and discuss each item on the list, and allow learners to mark up their own copies with notes about items they need to remember or mistakes they frequently make.

2. Have learners practice using the checklist when they write in class or for homework. (You can find a reproducible copy of the checklist in the Appendix E.)

3. Learners can use the checklist independently to check their own writing or pair up to check each other's writing.

2014 GED Test Editing Checklist:

1. Did I use the right words?
   - Check frequently confused words and homonyms: passed, past; it's, its; all ready, already; two, to, too; there, their, they're; knew, new, lose, loose; suppose, supposed to; through, threw, through; who, whom; lie, lay; lead, led.

2. Do my subjects and verbs agree?
   - Check singular or plural.

3. Do my pronouns (he, she, it, they) agree with their antecedents?
   - Check singular or plural.

4. Are modifiers in the correct order?
   - Check for dangling or misplaced modifiers.

5. Are important words capitalized?
   - Check first word in a sentence, proper nouns, and titles.

6. Did I use apostrophes correctly?
   - Check for apostrophes in possessive nouns.
   - Check for no apostrophes in plural nouns.

7. Did I use commas correctly?
   - Check clauses, series, and appositives.

8. Does every sentence have an end mark?
   - Check for periods, question marks, exclamation points.

9. Did I combine ideas and use conjunctions correctly?
   - Check for use of coordinating conjunctions (and, but, or, nor, for, so, yet).
   - Check for use of subordinating conjunctions (because, after, since, although, unless, until, etc.).

10. Are my ideas parallel?
    - Check that items compared or listed in a series have the same form.

11. Are my sentences clear and effective?
    - Check for repetitive words or awkward sentences.

12. Do my ideas follow a logical progression?
    - Check for use of transitional words and conjunctive adverbs to ensure logical order and clarity.

13. Did I correctly join or separate thoughts?
    - Check for run-on sentences or fused sentences.

14. Does every sentence contain a subject and verb?
    - Check for sentence fragments.

15. Did I select appropriate words?
    - Check for slang, nonstandard usage, informal words, or profanity.

SUGGESTION

After learners have used the checklist several times, ask if their writing has improved. Has using the checklist helped them to remember to check for these items before they turn in their assignments? Are there any items that they don't need to check for anymore? Discuss how using checklists regularly can help them to remember to correct the items on their own in their classwork and on the test.

Editing Grammar in Context

PURPOSE

To practice editing in context to prepare for the language skills drop-down menu items on the GED test.

METHOD

1. Prepare a nonfiction text related to your theme (about 400–900 words). Select several sentences within the text, and make them into drop-down menu items. You can do this in print or in a presentation. You can even write examples on the board. Each drop-down menu may contain a word, a phrase, or a whole sentence. You may choose to focus on just one or two grammar or mechanics issues if you are using this activity to practice or extend learning on a specific convention. If you are using this activity for general practice for the RLA Test, then you can make items that demonstrate a variety of the assessment targets (see Appendix A).

    If you can't model a drop-down item in class, leave a box or blank in the sentence. Then list four answer choices below or to the side.

2. Use the first paragraph or two to model the activity for students.

    Example sentence:

    > Tens of thousands of citizens signed a petition asking the governor not to cut funding to their local school districts.
    >
    > Example drop-down menu item:
    >
    > Tens of thousands of citizens signed a petition asking the governor not to cut funding to [Select... ▼] . local school districts.
    >
    >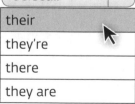
    >
    > | their |
    > | they're |
    > | there |
    > | they are |

3. Tell students that on the GED test, they will put the cursor on the "Select …" box and click the mouse. Then the answer choices will appear below in boxes. They will put the cursor on the correct answer choice and click. The answer will move to the correct place and complete the sentence or paragraph.

4. Ask a student volunteer to read the text question aloud.

5. Ask students which choice is correct and why? Have a student reread the sentence with the correct choice in place.

   Answer explanations:

   - Correct. "their" is the possessive plural, indicating the local school districts belong to the citizens.

   - Incorrect. "they're" is a contraction of *they are*.

   - Incorrect. "there" is a place.

   - Incorrect. "they are" makes no sense in the sentence.

6. Move on to the next drop-down item. Repeat the exercise as above. Make sure students reread each sentence and/or paragraph every time they select an answer.

7. If possible, show learners an example of what an actual drop-down item will look like on the test. You can show them the example in the Item Sampler (www.gedtestingservice.com/educators/itemsampler). Show students how they will select an answer, and then the answer will become part of the sentence. Remind them to always reread the sentence after they have selected the menu item to make sure that it is correct.

8. Ask students to complete the rest of the items individually or in small groups of 3 or 4. In groups, they should discuss and decide which answer is grammatically correct and explain why.

9. As a whole class, review the correct answers. Ask for students to recall the grammar rule or to explain why each answer is correct. Review rules and explanations as necessary.

SUGGESTION

This activity can be used to review grammar, usage, and/or mechanics. You can create mixed practice or focus on one skill. If you create a digital quiz, ideally learners should be able to select their answer from a drop-down menu embedded within the text so that they can see their answer in context.

6

The Mathematical Reasoning Test

Overview

The Mathematical Reasoning Test assesses the thinking skills that students use to solve math problems on tests and in real life. The test emphasizes a deep understanding of fundamental math concepts. Approximately 55 percent of test items will focus on algebraic problem solving while 45 percent will focus on quantitative problem solving, which includes number operations and geometric thinking.

Math Test items will require test-takers to use a variety of skills, including the following:

- Procedures: to know and be able to apply procedures

- Math fluency: to be able to use math accurately, efficiently, and flexibly

- Problem solving: to be able to use math reasoning to determine how to solve problems

Statistics and data interpretation will be assessed in quantitative problem solving, and the same concepts will also be assessed on the Science and Social Studies Tests.

The Math Test will be 90 minutes long and contain approximately 46 items. The test is split into two sections, but there is no break. Section one is a brief selection of items that do not allow the use of the calculator. Test-takers will be allowed to use the on-screen calculator in the second section. Multiple-choice items are worth 1 point each, but other item types may be worth 1, 2, or 3 points. The maximum point score for the test is 49 raw score points.

Item Types

A test item may stand alone, or two or three items may pertain to a stimulus such as a brief text, graph, table, geometric object, or graphic representation. Problems will be set in both academic and workplace contexts.

More than half of the test items will be traditional multiple-choice questions with four answer options. In addition, the test will include the following interactive item types:

- Fill-in-the-blank: Type a word or phrase to demonstrate mathematical reasoning or enter an equation to answer a problem. Mathematical symbols can be inserted using the symbol selector.

- Drop-down: Choose the correct answer from a drop-down menu embedded within a passage. Answers may include a word, numerical value, or comparison, such as less than, greater than, or equal to. When an answer is selected, it will appear on the screen as part of the text or equation.

- Hot spot: Click a sensor on the screen in order to select the correct answer on a coordinate plane, number line, dot plot, geometric figure, etc.

- Drag-and-drop: Use the mouse to drag small objects, words, or numerical expressions to targets on the screen. This might be used to properly sort data or to complete a graphic representation.

Approximately 20 percent of the items are at a cognitive complexity or DOK level one, 50 percent will be at level two, and 30 percent will be at level three.

Content

Approximately 30 percent of the math items will be aligned to a content standard as well as a mathematical practice. These reflect both the Common Core State Standards for math and the Process Standards published by the National Council of Teachers of Mathematics. The content indicators focus on math content and the specific skills that test-takers need to demonstrate.

Math assessment targets include two domains and four reporting categories:

1. Quantitative problem solving with
   - rational numbers: 25%
   - measurement: 20%

2. Algebraic problem solving with
   - expressions and equations: 30%
   - graphs and functions: 25%

The mathematical practices framework focuses on the math reasoning skills adults need to solve problems. They cover the following concepts:

- Planning a method and selecting appropriate math processes to solve problems

- Representing real-world problems using algebra

- Building or completing a line of reasoning

- Solving and displaying algebraic expressions with graphs

- Evaluating and correcting lines of reasoning

Assessment target content indicators for algebraic and quantitative problem solving and mathematical practices are listed in Appendix A.

Tools

Test-takers will be able to refer to a math formula sheet during the test. The formula sheet reflects the new test content and includes more algebraic formulas than the previous version. Some of the foundational formulas are no longer on the formula sheet, and test-takers will be required to remember them. Formulas that students will need to know by heart include:

- Area of squares and rectangles

- Perimeter of squares and rectangles

- Area and perimeter of triangles

- Circumference and area of circles

- Measures of central tendency

- Distance

- Total cost

Another tool available to test-takers is the onscreen calculator. The TI-30XS Multiview calculator will be available for use with most items on the Math Test as well as for some items on the Social Studies and Science Tests. Along with the calculator, students will be able to access a reference sheet that shows how to perform useful calculator operations. The TI-30XS is available for purchase as a handheld device for classroom practice. GEDTS offers video tutorials on using the calculator at www.gedtestingservice.com. Texas Instruments offers information about using the calculator and free calculator activities at www.atomiclearning.com/ti30xs.

A symbol selector tool will be available for test-takers to use when answering fill-in-the-blank items. See Appendix D for the symbol selector reference sheet, math formula sheet, and calculator reference sheet.

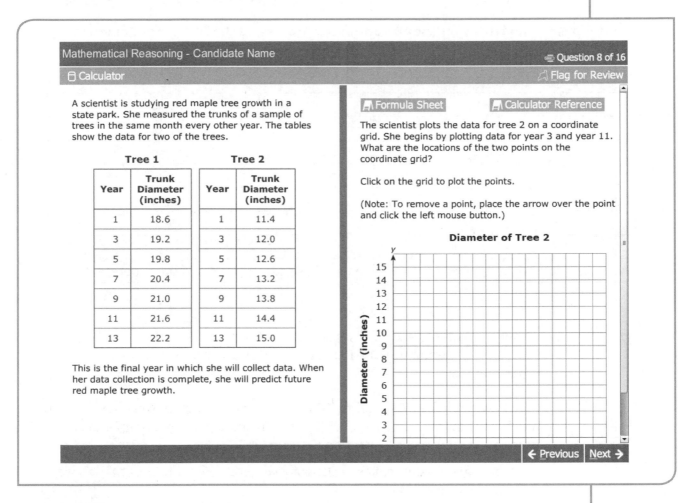

Answer Questions with Data Displays

Activity 38

PURPOSE

To show students how they can use graphs or other data displays to find answers to questions.

METHOD

1. Prepare and present a graph, chart, or other type of data display using presentation tools or handouts. Two samples are included here.

2. First, talk about how the graph or chart relates to your theme. For example: We have been discussing the economic situation in the U.S. Here is a chart from the U.S. Department of Health and Human Services. It shows the levels of income

for people and families who are at the federal poverty level. People who are at or below this level qualify for help from certain government programs.

2013 Poverty Guidelines for the 48 Contiguous States and the District of Columbia

People in family/household	Poverty guideline
1	$11,490
2	15,510
3	19,530
4	23,550
5	27,570
6	31,590
7	35,610
8	39,630

For families/households with more than 8 people, add $4,020 for each additional person.

3. Allow students to read the information in the chart. Answer any questions. Take time to define terms and explain the data so that students understand what it means.

4. Solicit questions. Ask students, "What questions do you have about this data and how it might relate to you?" You may need to give an example to get students started asking questions. Examples:

   a. If a single person makes $25,000 a year, what percentage is that above poverty level?

   b. What is twice, or 200%, of poverty level for a family of two?

   c. If a couple wants to be above poverty level, how much must each person make, if they make the same amount?

   d. If I make $12 an hour and I work 35 hours a week, am I above the poverty level? What if I am supporting two children?

5. After you have asked and answered several questions, talk about the data again. Ask, "Did asking and answering questions about the data help you to understand this chart better?"

6. Use this method to help students comprehend graphic information or data.

SUGGESTION

There are many sources of public data online. To find data and/or graphs that your students can relate to, go to government websites such as the Bureau of Labor Statistics (www.bls.gov), Department of Health and Human Services (www.hhs.gov), or www.data.gov.

Activity 39

Identify the Process

PURPOSE

To practice identifying the appropriate processes to use to solve mixed-practice problems.

METHOD

1. Create or find several mixed-practice problems. You may choose problems that use different combinations of processes, or you may want to focus on a particular set of processes, such as decimals and percents. You can make your own problem scenarios using stimuli that your students suggest or that they can relate to, such as:

    a. Find the perimeter and area of a rectangular park.

    b. The sub shop is hiring two workers at $8.75 per hour. How much will one employee make if he works 28 hours in one week? If the other worker works 35 hours, how much will the owner pay both of them for one week? For one year?

    c. A recipe calls for 1 pound of macaroni, 12 ounces of cheese, and 3 cups of milk. How much cheese and milk will you need if you use 1 ½ pounds of macaroni?

    d. Risa took two tests. She got 75% correct on the first test and 60% correct on the second. There were 170 questions on both tests combined. The second test had 10 more questions than the first. How many items did Risa answer correctly on each test?

2. You may choose to make the answer key available so that learners can check their own work. This is especially helpful if some individuals or pairs finish faster than others.

3. Explain the purpose of the activity to students: to determine the correct processes or operations to solve mixed-practice problems. Explain that each problem has multiple steps and that they will use more than one process. They may also need to use a process more than once.

4. Use a model problem to demonstrate the activity. Read the problem with learners and ask them which operations they think they would need to use to solve it. Then go through the process of solving the problem—with learners—step by step. Keep track of the processes you use. Talk about the problem-solving process. Were the learners right? Did they name all the required processes?

5. List the processes required to answer all the problems. You may generate this list yourself, or have learners look at the problems and guess which processes

they will use. If learners generate a list, make sure it is complete. Make a chart on the board or have learners make their own charts that show all the processes. Leave room to write problem numbers. For example:

Process	Problem Number
Addition	1, 2
Subtraction	1, 2
Multiplication	
Division	2

You may want to add other processes to the list, depending on what your lesson focus is. For example, reducing fractions, converting fractions to decimals, plotting points, using formulas, etc.

6. Have learners work in pairs or small groups to discuss and decide which processes they need to use to solve each problem. Have them complete their chart by putting the problem number next to each operation they need to use.

7. When all learners have categorized the problems, discuss the solutions together as a class. Ask learners what clues in each problem led them to the correct process. Keep track of the clues, and have learners make a list of clues for each operation.

SUGGESTIONS

•   If some learners finish early, allow them to check their own work and/or use the appropriate processes to find the solutions to the practice problems.

•   Give groups different problems to work on, and after they have identified the processes, have them trade problems. Then have the other groups complete the problems and check to see if the processes were correct.

Label the Steps

PURPOSE

To break real-world problems into small steps in order to find solutions.

METHOD

1. Find, create, or solicit from students two real-life problem scenarios that require math. Use one of the scenarios to model the activity for students. Here are some examples:

    a. How much will I make? Find a job ad that lists hourly pay or salary and answer questions about rate of pay per week, month, and year.

    b. How much does it cost? Use a store ad to calculate the total cost of items on a shopping list.

    c. Which is cheaper? Calculate and compare the costs of taking the bus and driving a car to work.

2. Tell students that this activity is about using math to solve problems and answer questions that they may come across in everyday life. Ask, "When do you use math?" (Possible answers: at the grocery store, at the gas station, at work, when I write a check, etc.)

3. Model the process for students. Use a projector or write the problem on the board. Demonstrate how to answer one of the questions. Work through the problem step by step. Label each step as you do it. Ask the class what to do next as you complete each step.

4. Ask individuals or pairs to solve the second problem, and to break it down into steps. The steps may include non-math steps, such as looking up information on the Internet or in a newspaper ad.

5. When students are finished, review their results. Have a student or pair of students demonstrate the steps they used to solve the problem. As they go through the process, ask the other students if they agree with each step, if they have anything to add, or if they did anything differently.

    See this example problem that GED students from Cleveland Community College completed:

Problem: Find the cost to get an associate's degree at the local community college.	
Step 1: Find important numbers.	Students look up the number of credits and cost per credit on the college website. Cost per credit: <u>$97.88</u> Number of credits required: <u>69 credits</u>
Step 2: Add, subtract, multiply, or divide?	Decide to <u>multiply</u> cost times credit to find the total.
Step 3: Put heavy number on top.	Set up the equation with the number with the least digits on the bottom: $97.88 × 69
Step 4: Multiply by 9.	Multiply 9 times each digit in 9788 and carry the tens: $97.88 × 69 —————— 88092
Step 5: 0 sits down.	Put 0 as a placeholder in the ones column of the next line: $97.88 × 69 —————— 88092 0
Step 6: Multiply by 6.	Multiply 6 times each digit in 9788 and carry the tens: $97.88 × 69 —————— 88092 587280
Step 7: Add results.	Add the two products and carry the tens: 88092 + 587280 —————— 675372
Step 8: Hop to the left.	Count the number of digits to the decimal point in the original numbers: 2 digits 675372
Step 9: Place the point.	Add the decimal point two digits from the right: 6753.72
Step 10: Give me that dollar!	Add the dollar sign: $6753.72.

TEACHING ADULTS: A GED® TEST RESOURCE BOOK

SUGGESTION

- Find a video, picture, or reading passage that presents a problem for students to address.

- Students can brainstorm or research additional real-life math problems. (For example: Find and compare the costs of two different vacations. Calculate gas money or bus fare, tolls, hotel bills, etc.)

Math Vocabulary: Writing Word Problems

PURPOSE

To practice using math vocabulary by writing word problems.

METHOD

Prepare by creating a math vocabulary list that relates to your lesson or unit. Include a brief definition and an example word problem, including each word that will remind students of what it means. You may want to ask students to help make a list and create examples of terms required for a lesson—either before or after the lesson. If you are using this activity before a lesson, make sure that students are already somewhat familiar with the terms. If you use this activity at the end of a lesson, students can review the vocabulary and practice using it by making their own lesson glossaries.

Explain the objective of the activity: to learn and remember math words by using them to write word problems.

Present the words one at a time. Ask students what each term means and to give an example of it. Provide definitions and gentle corrections, if required. Provide a word problem example for each term. Ask students to make up their own word problem for each term.

SUGGESTIONS

- Extend this activity by modeling how to solve each example word problem. Students can give the word problems to each other to solve, or you can compile their word problems into a worksheet for further practice.

- Combine this activity with Activity 42: Write Math Answers. Have students use the math terms to write problems, solve them, and then explain their answers.

Here is a list of math terms that GED students should be familiar with:

absolute value	elevation	manipulate	ray
acute	evaluate	matrix	quadratic equation
adjacent	event	mean	radius
arc	exponent	median	range
area	expression	midpoint	rate of change
average	factor	mode	ratio
binomial	formula	multiple	rational number
box plot	fraction	number properties	rectangle
chord	frequency	obtuse	right angle
circle	function	output	root
circumference	graph	percent	scale
coefficient	greatest common factor	perimeter	scalene
combination		periodicity	scientific notation
composite figure	histogram	permutation	slope
coordinate	inequality	perpendicular	square root
counterexample	input	plane	standard deviation
cube	integer	polygon	surface area
cube root	intercept	polynomial	symmetry
cylinder	interest	prism	translation
data	irrational number	probability	triangle
decimal	isosceles	proportion	unit rate
diameter	least common multiple	pyramid	unknown
dimension	like term	Pythagorean Theorem	variable
distributive property	linear expression	random	volume
dot plot			

Activity 42

Write Math Answers

PURPOSE

To give students a four-step process to use to understand and respond to math questions.

METHOD

1. Prepare a math word problem to use to model the problem-solving process. You can use this example problem or another problem that suits the needs of your students.

Problem: Divya's family took a trip to visit relatives in another state. The graph below shows information about distance and time on the trip.

What is the slope of the line?

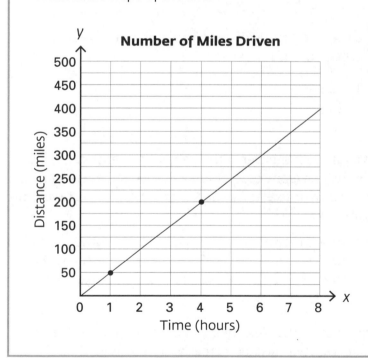

---

2. Tell your students they will use a four-step process to answer this question. Tell them that this is a good process to use with word problems. Some math problems on the GED test will not be multiple choice. They may have a box for you to type in your answer. This process will help you to understand the problem, calculate the correct answer, and know that your answer is correct.

    a. Step 1: Understand the problem

    b. Step 2: Think it through

    c. Step 3: Answer the question

    d. Step 4: Explain the answer

CHAPTER 6: THE MATHEMATICAL REASONING TEST

97

3. Step 1: Make sure students understand the problem. Review the information given in the problem and the graph. Ask:

   a. "How many miles did Divya's family drive in 1 hour?" (50)

   b. "What point on the graph shows this information?" (1, 50)

   c. "How many miles did Divya's family drive in 4 hours?" (200)

   d. "What point on the graph shows this information?" (4, 200)

4. Step 2: Ask, "What does the problem ask you to find?" (slope) Ask students if they remember the formula for slope. Tell them that if they don't, they can find the formula on the math formula sheet. During the Math Test, they will be able to click on an icon on the screen and look at the formula sheet. (See Appendix D: Math Tools for a copy of the formula sheet.) The formula for slope is:

$$m = \frac{y_2 - y_1}{x_2 - x_1}$$

   Now ask students to think about how to answer the question. "What do you need to know to find the slope?" (two points) You can use any two points to find slope.

5. Step 3: Tell students to use the two points given in the problem to write an equation for slope. Solve the equation.

$$m = \frac{200 - 50}{4 - 1} = \frac{150}{3} = 50$$

   The slope is 50.

6. Step 4: Ask students to explain their answer. This is a way students can check their thinking and be sure they have the correct answer. Instead of explaining their answer, they may also use a different method to calculate the answer and see if it's the same. For example:

   Slope is defined as rise over run. The rise is the change in the y-value, and the run is the change in the x-value. For these two points, I know that the rise is 200 – 50 = 150. I know that the run is 4 – 1 = 3. So, rise over run is 150 over 3 or 50.

   Tell students that rechecking or explaining their answers is a good way to be sure they are answering short-answer items correctly.

SUGGESTION

Use this process with word problems to get students used to analyzing problems and thinking about them before they solve them. Remind them that they can refer to the math formula sheet and the calculator reference sheet and use the calculator. They can also use their erasable noteboard to write and solve equations.

Activity 43

Math Matching

PURPOSE

To practice identifying and labeling expressions, data displays, or graphs.

METHOD

1. Select one or more expressions, charts, graphs, or other visuals for students to label. For example:

   a. Types of graphs: bar chart, number line, coordinate plane, pie chart, dot plot

   b. Equivalent fractions, decimals, and percents

   c. Names of geometric figures or names of parts of geometric figures

   d. Equations expressed in both numeral and text form, e.g., $A = \pi r^2$ matches "The area of a circle is π times radius squared."

2. Present students with the items to be matched. Display on the board or create a handout. Show students the item and the label names. Tell them that they need to put the labels in the correct place on the item. Students can write the labels in the correct place on a handout or place sticky notes on a visual display.

   Example:

circle

- diameter
- circumference
- radius

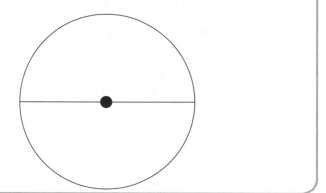

SUGGESTIONS

- Ask learners to define each label term.

- Use as a lesson preview or review activity to go over terms that are used in the lesson.

Activity 44

Graph a Text

PURPOSE

To practice graphing skills by creating graphic displays based on quantitative information from a text.

METHOD

1. Locate or prepare one or more text passages related to your theme or lesson.

2. Decide on which quantitative information to use for the graph. Produce a small sample text with that information marked and numbered to use as a model. Examples:

   a. Number of supporting details

   b. Number of words, sentences, or paragraphs

   c. Average number of words per sentence

   d. Number of quotes from each character

   e. Number of appearances of words from a vocabulary list

   f. Dates, quantities, or other numbers in the text

3. Select the type of graphic display you want learners to create, e.g., table, coordinate plane, bar graph, pie chart, line graph, etc. You may want to create a blank outline of the graphic for learners to fill in or supply learners with graph paper, if necessary. Create a key with the finished display.

4. Write detailed directions for learners to follow that tell them how to find and then graph the information. You can give learners the same text and directions and have them create different displays or have them all do the same display. Use the sample text to model the activity.

   Example directions:

   a. Read these three articles on the same theme. These examples are from *This I Believe* essays (www.thisibelieve.org) on the theme of community:

      ▹ "The Serenity to Change the Things I Can," by Mark Olmsted

      ▹ "This Is Home," by Majora Carter

      ▹ "The Farm That Binds," by Brenda

   b. Circle the main idea and underline supporting details in each essay.

   c. Count and record the number of supporting details and the number of paragraphs in each essay.

    d. Assign a variable to each of your data points:

- One variable for each essay title (*A*, *B*, *C*)
- Number of supporting details (*x*)
- Number of paragraphs (*y*)

    e. Represent this data mathematically, in three ways.

Table: Display data in a chart with 3 columns

Title	*x*	*y*
The Serenity to Change the Things I Can	5	8

Coordinate Plane: Graph point (*x*, *y*) for essays *A*, *B*, and *C*.

Bar Chart: Each bar should represent how many paragraphs are in an essay.

---

5. Explain the objective of the activity: to use numbers you find in a text to create your own graphic displays. Show students the model and explain the activity. Give students the text and directions.

6. Ask learners to read the text and create the graph(s).

7. Have students present their graphs to the class and describe how they created them.

SUGGESTIONS

- Learners will need to be familiar with a variety of graphic displays for the GED test. Consider having students create different displays for the same data so that the class can compare the displays. For example:

  - number line
  - dot plot
  - histogram
  - box plot
  - scatter plot

  - table
  - coordinate plane
  - bar graph
  - circle graph

- Have students graph numbers from their lives or their environment. Examples:

  - eye or hair color in the class: number of people with blue eyes, number of people with brown hair, etc.

> distance traveled to class: ask students how far they travel to get to class, how long it takes to get there, etc.

> other ideas: ages of children, years of birth, numbers of children or family members, etc.

Activity 45
Find the Data

PURPOSE

To practice finding the relevant data needed to solve a problem using an identified source.

METHOD

1. Select a word problem that fits your theme or topic. Leave out one quantity that will be necessary to solve the problem.

2. Present a source that students can use to find the data or quantity that they need to solve the problem. For example, write a word problem using data from one of these sources:

   a. Graphic from a newspaper article

   b. Almanac or weather statistics

   c. Project plan or blueprint

3. Model the activity by showing students a word problem with its source.

   Example:

   The distance between Chicago and Indianapolis is 165 miles. Jack lives in Chicago. He travels to Indianapolis and back home, and then he travels to Cincinnati. How many miles does Jack travel? How many miles will he travel if he goes from Indianapolis to Cincinnati without going back home?

   Provide a map or atlas for students to find the distance. Or let students look up the distance online.

4. Explain to students that they will have to find the data they need to complete the problems. Provide the source of the data or directions on how to access the source.

5. After students complete the problems, ask them to talk about how they found the data and explain the process they used to solve the problems.

SUGGESTIONS

- Allow students to access specific websites in order to find data. If you have computers in the class, bookmark the websites for students to use.

- Use Activity 41: Writing Word Problems and ask students to find data and write their own word problems. Students can exchange problems and solve them.

- Select a website, specialized web search portal, spreadsheet, or other large collection of data. Decide what data you want students to collect for a math challenge. For example, use data to make a graph or to write a word problem.

  ▷ Example: Ask students to find data on endangered species by the U.S. Fish & Wildlife Service (www.fws.gov) and make a graph that compares the numbers of three endangered animals. For more extensive searches, you can make this a group project that spans more than one class or is done outside of class.

Measurement: Practice with Fractions and Decimals

PURPOSE

To practice measuring with a ruler and converting measurements from fractions to decimals.

METHOD

1. Provide rulers and objects for each student to measure. For example, measure an orange, a book, a dollar bill, etc.

2. Talk about the ruler. Ask students to count how many lines are in one inch. (On most standard rulers there are 16.) Explain that this is the number of parts, so each line represents $\frac{1}{16}$. Draw a model of the ruler on the board. Write the sixteenths under each line.

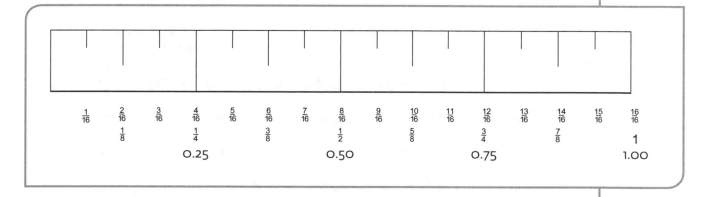

3. Now ask students to count how many medium lines are in one inch (eight). Write the eighths under the sixteenths. Ask students to reduce any fractions that they can. Mark quarters and halves.

4. Ask students to use the ruler to measure a small object, such as a button or coin. Ask them to write the answer using a fraction and to reduce the fraction, if possible.

5. Next ask students what one half of a dollar looks like written as a decimal ($0.50). Explain that one half of an inch can also be written as the decimal 0.50. Ask which fraction represents a quarter and how to write one or three quarters (0.25 and 0.75). Write the decimals underneath the fractions on the number line.

6. Ask students to measure another small object, this time using decimals. Explain how to convert eighths or sixteenths to a decimal. Tell students, "Divide the numerator by the denominator using a calculator or on paper." For example: $\frac{1}{8} = 1 \div 8 = 0.125$

7. Ask students to measure larger objects, such as a book or an orange. Tell them that to measure a round object like the orange, they can wrap a piece of string or paper around the orange and then measure the length of it. Model how to write measurements larger than one inch using fractions and decimals: $3\frac{1}{4}$" or 3.25"

SUGGESTION

Students can practice using calculators—even cell phone calculators—to convert measurements.

Measurement: Make a Graphic Organizer

PURPOSE

To practice measuring by following directions to create a graphic organizer.

METHOD

1. Write specific directions on the measurements required to make a graphic organizer. Make sure each student has a ruler, a pen or pencil, and a sheet of blank paper. Project, write on a board, or hand out the directions. Don't show students what the completed graphic organizer will look like before they start.

    Sample directions for a sequence graphic organizer with three parts:

    a. Place the paper lengthwise on the table, so the short side (8.5") is at the top.

    b. Measure 2 inches down from the top of the paper along the left and right sides. Make a small mark on each edge.

c. Place the ruler across the two marks and draw a line to connect them.

d. Measure 2 inches below the line and draw another line.

e. Measure 2 inches again and draw another line.

f. Measure 2 inches again and draw another line.

g. In the box at the top of the page, write "Topic:" and leave room to write in a topic later.

h. In the next box, on the left side, write the number 1.

i. In the box below that, on the left side, write the number 2.

j. In the box below that, on the left side, write the number 3.

k. Make an arrow that starts at number 1 and goes straight down to the number 2.

l. Make another arrow that starts at number 2 and goes straight down to the number 3.

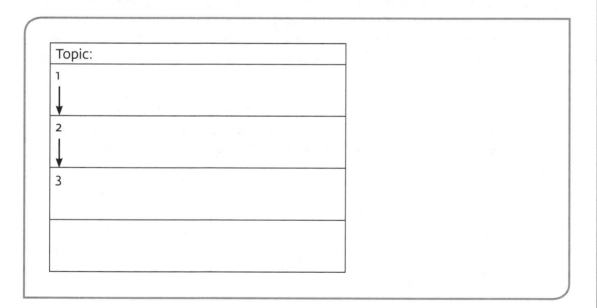

2. Explain that students will practice measuring by creating a diagram that they can use for another lesson.

3. Ask students to follow the directions step by step to make the graphic organizer.

4. When students are finished, ask them to compare their organizers. Do they all look the same? Small differences are acceptable, as long as the organizer still has three numbered boxes. If students did not successfully complete the organizer, show them a model created by you or another student, and have them redo the process either in class or as homework.

SUGGESTIONS

- Use two-sided rulers and give some measurements in metric units and others in inches.

- Prepare a text ahead of time that students can use to fill out the sequence chart when they have finished.

Activity

48

Geometry: Measure a Sphere

PURPOSE

To practice measuring and calculating the properties of a sphere.

METHOD

1. For this activity, you will need oranges or other round fruits, a knife, a cutting board, rulers, string, and scissors. Project or hand out the GED math formula sheet (see Appendix D). Cutting fruit can be messy, so be prepared! Bring paper towels, tablecloths, etc. Or you could use small balls from the dollar store. Be careful when cutting objects. You may want to cut the oranges in half yourself, before class.

2. Review the formulas for surface area and volume of a sphere on the formula sheet. Ask learners if they recall the formulas for circumference and area of a circle. Tell them that they will need to know these formulas by heart for the GED Math Test.

    - $c = \pi d$

    - $A = \pi r^2$

    - $SA = 4\pi r^2$

    - $V = \frac{4}{3}\pi r^3$

3. Give a half and a whole orange or ball to each learner or pair of learners. Make sure each learner or pair of learners has a ruler and a piece of string long enough to go around a whole orange.

4. Ask learners to use the ruler to measure the width across the cut side of the half orange. Ask learners, "What is this measurement?" (diameter) Have them write down the exact measurement. Example: diameter (d) = $3\frac{1}{4}$".

5. Explain that the radius (r) is half of the diameter. Ask learners to calculate the radius ($r = \frac{1}{2} d$). Then have them put the ruler on the orange so that they are measuring from the center of the face of the cut orange to the edge. Ask, "Did you get the same measurement for the radius?"

6. Ask learners to wrap the piece of string around the outside of the whole orange at its widest part. Have them mark the length of string it takes to go around it or cut the string to the exact length. Then have learners measure the piece of string. Ask, "What is this measurement?" (circumference) Have them write down the exact measurement. Example: circumference (c) = 11.5" (If you are using just halves of oranges, have learners measure the half-circumference and multiply by 2.)

7. Tell learners to calculate the diameter of the whole orange using the formula for circumference, and $\pi = 3.14$.

   Example:

   $c = \pi d$

   $11.5 = 3.14d$

   $3.66 = d$

8. You may have learners cut the oranges in half and check to see if the diameter is correct. Or provide them with cut oranges.

9. Have learners practice more formulas and calculations:

   a. area of a circle using the cut side of the orange

   b. surface area of the whole orange

   c. volume of the orange

SUGGESTION

If using real fruit is not possible, use virtual fruit. Hand out a sheet with drawings and diagrams showing a whole and a cut orange. Learners can measure the radius, diameter, and circumference using the drawings and a string.

Activity 49

Geometry: Measure 2D Paper Geometric Objects

PURPOSE

To practice measuring and calculating properties of geometric objects.

METHOD

1. Provide learners with pre-cut geometric shapes: triangles, rectangles, squares, parallelograms, trapezoids, and/or circles. Or print handouts with outlines of figures for learners to cut out. Make sure learners have rulers and copies of the math formula sheet (see Appendix D). Provide or display other formulas as needed.

2. Ask learners to cut out the figures (if needed). Then ask them to name each figure. If the figures are paper, they can write the names on them. If the figures are manipulatives, have students write the names on sticky notes.

3. Ask, "Where do you see these figures in the real world?" Examples: yield signs are triangles, speed limit signs and books are rectangles, clocks are circles, etc.

4. Look at the formula sheet. Ask learners to match the formulas on the sheet to the figures. "What shape goes with this formula?" (parallelogram, trapezoid) Ask, "What formulas do you know for the other figures?" (area and perimeter of rectangle and square, circumference and area of circle, area and perimeter of triangle). Review the formulas that are not on the formula sheet. Make sure learners understand that they will need to memorize these formulas for the GED Math Test. Review the variables and formulas (for example, b = base, h = height, Area $A = bh$).

5. Ask learners to label the variables on the figures.

6. Have learners use the labeled figures to practice measuring and calculating perimeter and area.

SUGGESTIONS

- For more work with real-world geometric figures, find or take photos—or have learners take photos—of different shapes.

- Ask learners to make a flashcard for each figure that shows a drawing of the figure with labeled parts and its formulas.

- Extension activity: Ask learners to use the shapes to create composite figures. Measure and calculate perimeter and area of the composites. Show drawings or photos of real-world composite figures, such as houses. See if learners can deconstruct the figures into their parts.

Activity 50

Geometry: Calculating with 3D Paper Geometric Objects

PURPOSE

To build conceptual understanding of 3D geometric shapes by creating and manipulating them.

METHOD

1. Create and/or copy patterns and directions for making 3D shapes from paper. There are many online sources for these, such as www.fun-stuff-to-do.com. Provide students with patterns, directions, scissors, and glue or tape. You may choose to focus on just one figure or to discuss several at once and compare them.

2. Provide handouts or project the math formula sheet (see Appendix D). Review the formulas for surface area and volume of 3D figures.

3. Ask learners to cut out and assemble one of the shapes. Ask if students know the name of the figure (for example, this is a pyramid).

4. Ask, "Where do you see these figures in the real world?" Examples: the pyramids in Egypt, ice cream cones, soup cans, boxes, etc.

5. Look at the formula sheet. Ask learners to match the formulas on the sheet to the figures. "Which object goes with this formula?" (prism, cylinder, pyramid, cone, sphere) Ask, "What do you need to know to calculate the surface area of a pyramid?" (perimeter of the base, area of the base, slant length). Ask, "What is the perimeter of the base of this pyramid?" (Students measure the base and calculate perimeter.) Ask, "What is the area of the base?" (Students calculate the area.) Ask, "What is the slant? What is the length of the slant?" (Students point to the slant and measure it.) Have learners calculate the surface area of the pyramid. Follow the same procedure to calculate volume.

6. You may move on and use the same procedure to calculate surface area and volume of other figures. Or you may want to focus your work on one figure and continue to practice with it.

SUGGESTIONS

- Bring in real objects, such as cans and ice cream cones. Have learners measure them and calculate surface area and volume.

- Extend this activity by creating composites (two or more adjacent figures) and calculating the surface area or volume.

- Ask learners questions that require them to use measurements and formulas for 3D objects.

    a. How much paper is required for the label of a soup can?

    b. How much does the Earth weigh?

    c. How much paint do you need to buy to paint the house?

    d. How big a piece of cardboard do you need to make a pizza box?

The Science Test

Overview

The GED Science Test measures science reasoning skills and the ability to apply these skills in realistic situations. Content focuses on three content domains: life science, physical science, and Earth and space science. Stimulus materials may include a brief text, diagram, graph, table, or other graphic representation of data or scientific concepts.

Test-takers will be required to analyze, understand, and extract information from scientific text, make inferences and predictions based on scientific data, and solve problems by applying scientific theories and processes.

The Science Test will be 90 minutes long and include approximately 34 questions worth a total of 40 raw score points. Multiple-choice items are worth 1 point each, but other item types may be worth 2 or 3 points. There will be two short-answer items scored on a 3-point scale. Answers may be scored holistically or analytically, depending on the requirements of the prompt. For example, if a question requires three specific details for a complete response, test-takers may receive one point for each correct detail. If a question requires a more general answer, then scoring guides will be used to determine the score.

Item Types

A test item may stand alone, or two or three items may pertain to a stimulus such as a brief text, graph, or diagram. About half of the test items will be traditional multiple-choice questions with four answer options. In addition, the test will include the following interactive item types:

- Fill-in-the-blank: Type a word or phrase to define an idea or describe a trend on a graph.

- Drop-down: Choose the correct answer from a drop-down menu embedded within a passage. Answers may include words or phrases that complete a sentence. When an answer is selected, it will appear on the screen as part of the text or equation.

- Hot spot: Click a sensor on the screen in order to select the correct answer on a graph, chart, or diagram.

- Drag-and-drop: Use the mouse to drag small objects, words, or data to targets on the screen. This might be used to properly sort data or to complete a graphic representation.

- Short answer: Summarize, provide a hypothesis or conclusion, or cite evidence to support a particular conclusion. Suggested time for each short answer is 10 minutes, but test-takers will need to manage their own time.

Approximately 80 percent of the items will involve a cognitive complexity or DOK level of two or three. The rest of the items will be at level one.

Content

Content focuses on two main themes: "Human Health and Living Systems" and "Energy and Related Systems." The test will cover three major domains:

- Life science (40%): human body and health, structure and function of life, molecular basis for heredity, evolution, relationships between life functions and energy intake, ecosystems

- Physical science (40%): chemical properties and reactions related to human systems; conservation, transformation, and flow of energy; work, motion, and forces

- Earth and space science (20%): interactions between Earth's systems and living things, Earth and its system components and interactions, structure and organization of the cosmos

Science assessment targets are derived from CCSS for Literacy in Science & Technical Subjects, CCSS for Mathematics, and the National Research Council's A Framework for K-12 Science Education. Eight science practices are used to guide the assessment of scientific reasoning:

1. Comprehending scientific presentations

2. Investigation design, through both experiment and observation

3. Reasoning from data

4. Evaluating conclusions with evidence

5. Working with findings

6. Expressing scientific information

7. Scientific theories

8. Probability and statistics

Complete science assessment targets are listed in Appendix A.

Stress Management: Breathing

PURPOSE

To teach students a breathing technique that can help them stay relaxed and focused.

METHOD

1. Introduce the topic of breathing. Ask, "What happens when you breathe?" See if learners can describe the process:

    a. Inhalation: Oxygen goes in the mouth or nose and into the lungs.

    b. Oxygen flows from the lungs into the capillaries, entering the bloodstream and flowing to cells throughout the body.

    c. At the same time, carbon dioxide comes into the lungs from the bloodstream.

    d. Exhalation: The carbon dioxide is then expelled from the lungs out the mouth and nose.

2. Tell students that they will learn a breathing relaxation technique that they can use during the GED test—or any time—to lower their stress. Tell them that breathing deeply sends a message to the brain to calm down. When the body gets this message, heart rate slows and blood pressure goes down.

3. Read the breathing for relaxation technique aloud to students:

    a. Sit in a comfortable position with your feet on the ground.

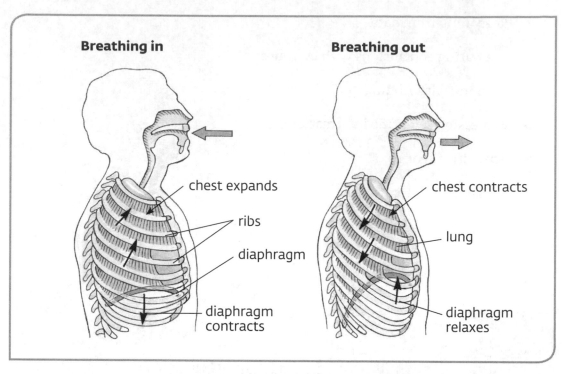

Breathing in   **Breathing out**

chest expands

ribs

diaphragm

diaphragm contracts

chest contracts

lung

diaphragm relaxes

b. Put one hand on your belly just below the ribs and the other hand on your chest.

c. Take a deep breath in through the nose. You should feel your belly expand. Your chest should not move.

d. Now breathe out through pursed lips like you are whistling. You should feel the hand on your belly move in as the air is pushed out.

e. Focus on your breathing and repeat this exercise two more times.

4. Ask students how they feel after the breathing exercise. If they want to continue, have them take three more deep breaths. Tell them that when they feel stressed, they can take three to 10 deep breaths until they feel their bodies begin to relax.

5. Discussion questions:

a. How do you feel after focusing on your breathing?

b. What is happening when you breathe? (Oxygen is coming into your lungs, then through your bloodstream to your cells. Carbon dioxide is going from the cells through the bloodstream to your lungs, and then out.)

c. Can you feel any changes in your body when you are breathing deeply?

d. How could this exercise help if you are dealing with a stressful situation like an important test?

6. Review the breathing diagram with students. Have them breathe while looking at the diagram and trace the path of the air on the diagram.

7. Remind students to add new vocabulary to their class notes or personal dictionaries.

SUGGESTION

If students want to know more about respiration and how the body uses oxygen to make energy, have them research it online. (You can read a good overview of the process on respiration.net.)

Use a Punnett Square to Predict Traits

PURPOSE

To use a Punnett square to determine the probability of traits.

METHOD

1. Prepare by creating or reproducing a handout of a Punnett square for students. Project or display a Punnett square to use as a model for the activity.

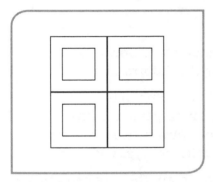

2. Explain that students will use a Punnett square to determine the probability of a trait being passed on from parents to their children. Hand out or show students a blank Punnett square. Explain that it is a diagram that helps predict possible genetic outcomes when two individuals mate.

3. Ask students, "What traits did you get from your parents?" Talk about similarities between parents and their children and between siblings.

4. Discuss and demonstrate the model Punnett square:

    a. This diagram shows the traits for curly hair and straight hair.

    b. Curly hair is recessive. That means you need two small c's—one from each parent—to have curly hair. Straight hair is dominant. That means you only need one big C to have straight hair. A child with Cc or CC will have straight hair. (Define vocabulary as necessary.)

    c. A woman with curly hair—see the two small c's on the left side of the square?—has children with a man who has straight hair—see the big C and little c on the top of the square?

d. The four possible outcomes for their children are shown in the four small squares.

e. Look at the first small square. It gets a big C from Dad and a little c from Mom. Will this child have straight hair or curly hair? (straight) Why? (because the big C is dominant)

f. Look at the rest of the possible children. How many of them have straight hair? (2) How many have curly hair? (2)

g. What is the probability that a child of these two parents will have straight hair? (50%) Curly hair? (50%)

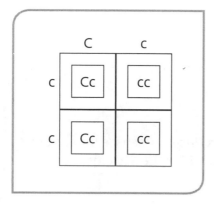

5. After students have talked about the model and understand how it works, ask them to complete their own Punnett square using this information:

a. Black hair (B) is homozygous dominant (BB = black). Brown hair (Bb) is heterozygous (Bb = brown). Blonde hair (b) is homozygous recessive (bb = blonde). If necessary, explain that homozygous means two of the same types (BB or bb) and heterozygous means two different types (Bb).

b. A brown-haired woman marries a brown-haired man. They are expecting a child.

c. Use the Punnett square to determine the probability of the child having black hair, brown hair, or blonde hair. Express the probabilities as percents.

Answer shown below:

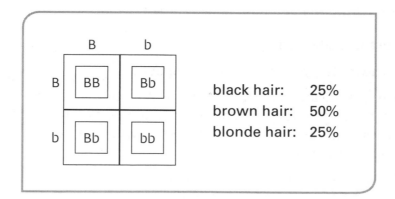

6. As a class, compare student answers, and discuss the diagrams. If some students answered incorrectly, have a student who answered correctly describe how she filled out the diagram and got the answer.

SUGGESTIONS

- Extend this activity for higher level students by adding more details about genotypes (genetic codes that determine traits in an organism) and phenotypes (physical characteristics of an organism).

- For more work with Punnett squares, use attached vs. free-hanging earlobes, freckles, and other traits.

Activity 53
Experiment: Does Writing Help Memory?

PURPOSE

Design an experiment to test the hypothesis that writing down information helps students recall it.

METHOD

1. Explain the purpose of the activity: to design an investigation to test if writing something down helps students recall information later.

2. Discussion questions to gauge previous knowledge:

   a. What is a scientific investigation? (It is the process of observing, making a hypothesis, experimenting to test the hypothesis, and making a conclusion that may or may not validate the hypothesis.)

   b. What is a hypothesis? (It's an educated guess—something that you think might be true, based on information you have observed.) A hypothesis is untested. We test hypotheses through either experiments or observations.

   c. What are independent and dependent variables? (Independent variables are the things you think are the cause, and dependent variables are the effects you are trying to test.)

3. Ask students if they can think of a way to test this hypothesis:

   Does writing information down help students remember it later?

4. Facilitate discussion about what steps students could take to design the experiment. Start with brainstorming: There are no bad ideas. Do not make too many suggestions.

5. Once students have brainstormed a list of ideas, ask them to vote on which one idea they should use for their experiment.

6. After they have made a decision, ask clarifying questions about the specifics. For example, "So you want to make a quiz to give now and later. What should the quiz be about? How much later will you give it the second time? Who will you give the quiz to? What are the variables?" Write the details of the experiment on the board or have a student write them.

7. Review the order of the steps to make sure that they make sense. Ask, "Are these steps in the correct order?" Have students discuss and decide on the order of the steps and modify the list if necessary. Review the steps, and modify or suggest modifications, if necessary.

Example experiment:

Step 1	Create a list of 10 pieces of information.
Step 2	Write the list on the board and ask 20 students to look at it.
Step 3	Have 10 of the people copy the list on paper. Have the other 10 people just look at it without writing. When the copiers are finished, erase or cover the list and take away the papers.
Step 4	Wait 15 minutes. Then ask people to remember the 10 things on the list and write them on a piece of paper.
Step 5	Look at the papers and find the average number of items each group remembered.

8. Walk students through the process of conducting the investigation. For this example, some students may create the list of items while other students do a different activity.

9. Compare and discuss the results. Ask, "Did this prove or disprove the hypothesis? Did the students who copied the list remember more?" Ask, "What do the results of your experiment mean?"

10. Post-experiment discussion:

    a. "When studying or taking notes from a class discussion, what type of information do you write down? What do you want to remember?"

    b. "Are there any study habits that you use and want to share? What helps you remember information?"

SUGGESTION

Have additional activities ready for students who are not conducting tasks during different parts of the investigation. You could extend this activity by giving waiting students related stories or articles to read about topics like memory, good study habits, or learning styles.

Activity

54

Can You See the Music?

PURPOSE

To visualize sound waves using an oscilloscope.

METHOD

1. Search for free oscilloscope software or an oscilloscope app for a computer or mobile device you have available in class. Download the software or app so that you can project it for the class or show it to students.

2. Select a song or have learners suggest a song to use for the experiment. There are many websites that offer free music, or you can use music that you already have on your computer or mobile device.

3. Test out the app before class so that you know how to see the oscilloscope and simultaneously play the music.

4. Create or find a model of a wave that shows wavelength, amplitude, crest, and trough.

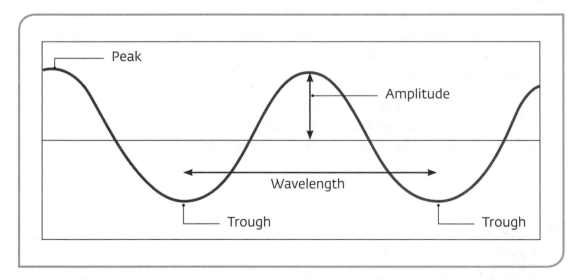

5. Explain that you are going to use an oscilloscope to look at sound waves.

6. Ask, "Have you ever seen sound waves? What do you know about waves? What other kinds of waves are there?" (light waves, water waves, shock waves, etc.) Ask, "Do you know what frequency is?" (the rate at which something occurs or repeats) Demonstrate what frequency is by showing samples of high and low frequency sound waves.

7. Open the oscilloscope and project or show it to the class. Tell students that any sounds they make may be picked up by the oscilloscope. When students are

quiet, play the song and ask students to silently observe the waves. After the song is over, ask them to write about what they saw.

8. Discuss students' descriptions of the sound waves. How are they similar or different? Have students read what they wrote.

9. If students want more information, discuss details about the sound waves. Ask:

   a. "What is sound?" (pressure that moves back and forth in waves)

   b. "What is frequency?" (how fast the waves move; the faster the waves move, the higher the sound)

   c. "What is wavelength?" (the distance between the start and end of one wave; in other words, how long it takes a wave to go all the way up to the top, down to the bottom, and back to the center)

   d. "What are the crest and the trough?" (the highest and lowest points of the wave)

   e. "What is amplitude?" (the distance between the center and the crest)

10. Wrap up with discussion of who might need to know or use sound waves or oscilloscopes. (Examples: musicians, producers, scientists, sound technicians, construction workers, architects, interior designers, etc.)

SUGGESTIONS

- The key vocabulary terms students need for the GED Science Test include: waves, frequency, wavelength, amplitude, crest, and trough. Have students create their own drawing of waves with labels for the terms as a study tool.

- Ask students to predict how high pitch sound, low pitch sound, or their own voices might look in the oscilloscope. Have them draw the wave pattern that they predict, and then use the oscilloscope to see if they are correct.

Activity
55

Write a Timed Short Answer to a Science Prompt

PURPOSE

To practice writing quick responses to sample Science Test items.

METHOD

1. Prepare a short answer question connected to your theme. See the Science Item Sampler or the Assessment Guide for sample questions (www.gedts.com).

The prompt should require no longer than 10 minutes for students to write a complete answer. Prompts should be based on brief text passages and/or graphic information. Some ideas for science short-answer questions include:

    a.   Design an experiment based on a scenario.

    b.   Describe features of a natural object and what those features mean to scientists.

    c.   List and describe three stages in a process, in the correct order.

2. Explain the objective of the activity: to read and respond to a science prompt correctly within 10 minutes. Assure learners that this is a learning activity, not a test, but it is designed to get them comfortable with answering these types of questions quickly.

3. Provide the stimulus material and the prompt. Tell learners that you will time them.

4. Have learners begin. Start timing. Tell them when five minutes have passed. When 10 minutes have passed, tell learners. Ask how many are finished. Allow learners a few more minutes to finish, but keep track of how long it takes.

5. Discuss the answer. Have learners volunteer to read their answers. If a learner has the correct, complete answer, tell him he would get 3 points. Tell learners that they can get 0, 1, 2, or 3 points for their answer. Ask, "What does this mean?" (It means that even if they are not sure of the complete answer, they should write what they know because they may get 1 or 2 points for trying.)

6. Ask learners if they think they could answer another question in only 10 minutes. Discuss the timing. "How did it make you feel to know that you were supposed to answer in such a short time?" Explain that on the test, there will be a clock on the screen, but that they do not have to stop after 10 minutes. That is just the suggested time in order for them to have enough time for all the questions on the test. Tell learners that are more nervous looking at the clock that they will be able to hide the clock on the computer screen during the test.

SUGGESTION

Use Activity 36: Using an Editing Checklist to have learners check for errors in the responses. Tell students that with short answers, writing the complete answer is more important than grammar or mechanics, but they should still try to write clearly and correctly.

8

The Social Studies Test

Overview

The GED Social Studies Test focuses on the fundamental reasoning skills necessary to analyze and understand information that represents a broad range of social studies content. Test items cover civics, U.S. history, economics, and world geography. Stimulus materials include primary source documents as well as secondary sources and may consist of text, maps, graphs, tables, or other graphic representations of data.

With the addition of the extended response item, test-takers are required to demonstrate a deep, conceptual understanding of overarching social studies themes as well as be able to analyze evidence from source texts in order to present and defend a written argument using specific and relevant details.

The Social Studies Test is 90 minutes long and includes approximately 35 questions. Multiple-choice items are worth 1 point each, but other item types may be worth 2 or 3 points. There is one extended response worth 8 points, the balance of the test is worth 36 raw score points, and the total test has a maximum point total of 44 raw score points.

The Social Studies Test begins with a 65-minute section that includes a variety of item types. The second section is a separately timed extended response item. When the extended response begins, the test-taker will have 25 minutes to type a response and will not be able to return to the first part of the test. Any extra time left after the first part of the test is not added to any other part of the test.

Item Types

More than half of test items will be multiple-choice questions with four answer options. The test also includes a variety of technology-enhanced, interactive test items:

- Drag-and-drop: Use the mouse to move small images, words, or numerical expressions to drop targets on the screen. This might be used to properly classify, sort, or order items.

- Drop-down: Choose the correct word or phrase from menu options embedded within a passage. The selected answer will appear on the screen to complete a logical conclusion or generalization.

- Fill-in-the-blank: Type a word or phrase to demonstrate understanding of a concept, term, or graphical representation.

- Hot spot: Click a sensor on the screen in order to select the correct answer on a graph, chart, or map.

- Extended response: Type a response to a prompt based on one or more passages, citing evidence from the passage(s) and using standard English conventions.

Approximately 80 percent of the items will involve a cognitive complexity or DOK level of two or three. The rest of the items will be level one.

Content

Content focuses on two main themes: "Development of Modern Liberties and Democracy" and "Dynamic Responses in Societal Systems." The test covers four major content domains:

- Civics and Government (50%): types of modern and historical governments, principles that have contributed to American democracy, structure and design of U.S. government, individual rights and civic responsibilities, American politics, contemporary public policy

- United States History (20%): historical documents that have shaped American government, revolutionary and early republic periods, Civil War and Reconstruction, civil rights, European settlement and population of the Americas, World War I, World War II, the Cold War, American foreign policy since 9/11

- Economics (15%): key economic events that have shaped American government and policies, political and economic freedoms, fundamental economic concepts, micro- and macro-economics, consumer economics, economic causes and impacts of wars, economic drivers of exploration and colonization, scientific and industrial revolutions

- Geography and the World (15%): classical civilizations, relationships between the environment and societal development, borders between peoples and nations, human migration

Complete social studies assessment targets are listed in Appendix A.

Activity 56 — Reader's Theater

PURPOSE

To bring historic characters and events to life by acting out a history passage.

METHOD

1. Select a history passage that describes events and the people who were key figures in those events. Examples:

    a. The creation of the bill of rights

    b. Lincoln's speech on the emancipation proclamation

    c. The women's suffrage movement

    d. Thomas Jefferson and the Declaration of Independence

2. Divide the text into parts, either by character or by sections. If a text has only one character or voice, you can break it up so that one student reads the first part, then another reads the next section, etc. Or you could have two or three students read the same speech, one after the next, as a fluency activity. Assign parts to students or have them volunteer. You can do this as a class or have several small groups act out the same piece.

3. Allow readers to practice with their groups or to pre-read the text before reading with the class.

4. Ask each group of students to act out the text for the rest of the class. If they want to use props or dress up, allow them time to prepare. Help them with the correct pronunciation of words they are not familiar with and help them to define new vocabulary. Ask students to be as creative as possible to bring the text to life.

5. Once they are prepared, let the students take the stage!

6. After the performance(s), have the audience members respond and ask questions.

SUGGESTION

If you have a very confident and creative group, you can divide the class into small groups and give a different text to each group to perform. This works well with a series of texts that tell a story or sequence of events such as a pre-Civil War story, a battle story from the war, and a post-war reconstruction story or event.

Activity 57

Who Represents You?

PURPOSE

To identify elected officials at the local, state, and federal levels and understand what they do.

METHOD

1. Identify websites where your learners can search for their local and state legislatures or other elected bodies, such as Find Your Representative at www.house.gov or your local city, town, or county website.

2. Select one or two offices at each level of government for learners to research. You can connect this to your theme in many ways. For example, if you are working on an Earth Science unit about natural resources, you may choose to have learners find which elected official represents them with legislation that impacts their local environment.

    Note: There are over 500,000 elected officials at the state and local levels!

3. Create a handout or write on the board information for students to complete with one or two seats at each level of government. For example:

    •   U.S. House of Representatives

    •   State Board of Education

    •   City/Township/Village Board of Education

4. Explain the activity to learners. Tell them that they will find out the names, positions, and contact information of some of their elected officials.

5. Introductory discussion questions:

    a. What experience do you have with elected government representatives? Have you seen them speak on TV or in person? Have you read mail from an official or a candidate?

b. Have you voted in an election? What types of government positions have you voted for? What is the difference between voting for the president and voting for the mayor?

c. What are the three levels of government? (federal, state, and local) How are they similar or different? What do officials do at each level? How are they similar or different?

6. Ask if anyone knows the name of one of their representatives (or their mayor, or any of their local officials, such as a county executive or a town court judge). Learners may live in different districts and have different representatives and officials. Talk about officials in your district, and give examples of how you know about and hear about or from them.

7. Demonstrate how to go to one of the websites to find a representative. For example, go to Find Your Representative at www.house.gov and enter your own zip code. (The name and photo of your congressional representative appear alongside a map of your district.) Ask learners to enter their zip codes, or enter them while students watch.

8. Show learners how to find the rest of the information, and either give them time to work or assign it as homework.

9. Share the results with the class. Discuss the results. Ask, "How many of you wrote Congresswoman Roby?" See how many officials your students have in common and how many are different. Ask if learners have ever seen, met, or heard any of the officials. Ask if any students voted for the officials on their lists.

10. Continue the discussion with questions like these:

a. If you talked to these representatives, what would you want to ask them? What would you tell them is important to you?

b. How could you find out where your representative stands on the issues that are important to you?

c. Does the website say how you can contact these representatives? Would you like to contact your representative?

SUGGESTION

If some learners complete the activity earlier than others, provide some of the conclusion discussion questions for them to research on the website.

Activity 58

Make Your Voice Heard: Write Your Representative

PURPOSE

To express opinions about current issues by writing a letter to an elected representative.

METHOD

1. You may want to use this activity after Activity 57: Who Represents You? When learners locate the names of their representatives, have them copy the contact information.

2. Show learners a sample formal letter to a representative. (You can find sample letters online at state and local websites like www.scstatehouse.gov.) Discuss the parts of the letter and how it is formatted. Explain that a letter to an official is written like a persuasive essay. Talk about the parts that the letter will include:

   a. An introduction: who you are, why you are writing, what you want

   b. Details about your position on an issue and your request, facts and details to support your request

   c. A conclusion that sums up your request and thanks the representative for his/her time

Here is an example of how to address a letter to a representative:

If writing to members of the U.S. House of Representatives:	Date The Honorable (full name), United States House of Representatives (get street address here: forms.house.gov/wyr/welcome.shtml), Washington, DC 20515 Dear Representative (last name):
If writing to members of the U.S. Senate:	Date The Honorable (full name), United States Senate (get street address here: www.senate.gov/general/contact_information/senators_cfm.cfm), Washington, DC 20510 Dear Senator (last name):

3. Tell learners that they will write letters to their own elected representatives about an issue they are interested in. Or present learners with a text passage about an issue—current or past—and have them write a letter about it. For instance, have them write letters to President Lincoln expressing their views on slavery and telling him what they want him to do about it. Or have them write to President Obama about their views on health care reform.

4. Direct learners to draft their letters. Allow them to refer to the sample letter and the list of parts they should include. Remind them to include specific details and to describe how the issue affects them personally.

5. After learners have written their drafts, allow time for review. Either review the letters yourself and give suggestions for improvements or have learners work in pairs to review each other's letters. Tell them that it helps to have someone else read their letters to see if they have made their points clearly. Give learners time to revise their letters either in class or as homework.

6. After learners are finished with their letters, ask volunteers to read their letters to the class. Be supportive and encouraging. Praise students for using details to support their positions, citing particular current events or legislation, and for using precise vocabulary. Ask clarifying questions, if they are necessary. Tell learners that they can still revise their letters to make their points clear before sending them, if they choose.

SUGGESTIONS

- Use Activity 36: Using an Editing Checklist to have learners correct errors and revise their letters.

- Ask if learners want to send the letters. If they do, discuss whether to use email or postage. Help them to address and send their letters.

- Organize a field trip to the local office of an elected official. Have learners present letters to the official in person.

Activity 59

Geography: Where in the World?

PURPOSE

To identify locations on a world map.

METHOD

1. Identify locations around the world (or on a national, state, or local map) relevant to your theme, unit, or lesson. Example: Find locations where major historical events occurred or find where a historical figure lived.

2. You will need world map, a globe, or the ability to project a map using your computer. You may also find relevant maps in textbooks or library books.

3. Present the background material. For example, discuss the division of Germany and the erection and destruction of the Berlin Wall.

4. Ask students to identify on the map the place where they think the event took place. For instance, if you are discussing the Berlin Wall, first show a map of Europe. Ask students to point out Germany. Then ask them if they know where the wall was. After some discussion, show students a map of Germany that shows the outline of the wall.

5. Another way to present this is to use Google Maps. Start with a map of Europe. Then zoom in on Germany. You can then focus in on the wall, and even focus in on a photo of the Berlin Wall Memorial site in Berlin.

SUGGESTIONS

- Use the map activity as a starting point for discussion on your topic. Show students or have them find the place where the events happened.

- You can also use this activity as a lesson review to assess if students understand and can find where the events took place.

Activity
60

What Does the Political Cartoon Mean?

PURPOSE

To use visual literacy skills to analyze a political cartoon.

METHOD

1. Find two or more political cartoons related to your theme. Search your local news site (especially for current events), or try one of these other sources:

   a. Daryl Cagle's Political Cartoons at www.cagle.com

   b. Library of Congress at www.loc.gov (teachers > classroom materials > themed resources > political cartoons)

   c. Cartoons in the Classroom at Newspapers in Education at www.nieonline.com

2. Choose one cartoon to use as an example. Project or display it for the class. Ask learners to look at the parts of the cartoon:

   a. What is the cartoon about? Can you tell what the topic is?

   b. Who are the characters? Are there people in the cartoon? Who are they? If there are animals, what do the animals represent?

   c. What is happening in the cartoon? What are the people doing or saying?

3. Discuss the meaning of the cartoon with learners.

4. Present another cartoon to learners or give them a link to the cartoon online. Have learners work in pairs or small groups to answer these questions:

   a. What is the topic? (Look at the caption, labels, or dialogue.)

   b. Who are the characters? (Are they famous people? Do the characters represent someone or something else?)

   c. What is the situation? (Where are the characters? What is happening? What are the characters saying?)

   d. How does the cartoon relate to the news or a political issue?

   e. What is the message? (What is the cartoonist saying about the topic or character?)

   f. Do you agree or disagree with the cartoonist?

5. After groups have had a chance to discuss the cartoon, come together with the whole class and discuss. Ask someone from each group to explain what the cartoon is about. If learners disagree or do not know, facilitate the discussion.

6. Ask learners if they think the cartoonist is trying to persuade them to believe or do something. Ask, "What is the cartoonist's motive? Why did he or she draw this cartoon?"

7. Finally, have learners write a brief summary of what the cartoon means.

SUGGESTIONS

- Challenge learners to use a template or online cartoon creator to make their own cartoons about a situation or issue they care about.

- Bring in local newspapers and discuss editorial cartoons that are relevant to your town or state. If learners feel strongly about the opinion expressed in a cartoon, they may want to write a letter to the editor explaining their feelings.

Activity
61

Make a Time Line

PURPOSE

To use a time line to visualize a sequence of events.

METHOD

1. Prepare by assembling a list of events that relate to your theme or topic. Print enough blank time lines and copies of the list of events for each student, pair, or small group. Cut each list into strips with one event per strip. Gather the strips in envelopes or with paper clips. Give each student or group a complete

TEACHING ADULTS: A GED® TEST RESOURCE BOOK

set of event strips and one blank time line. If you choose, you could create a digital time line for students to drag and drop the events in the correct order.

Here is a sample list of events for voting amendments to the U.S. Constitution:

1804 Amendment 12	States choose electors to vote for president and vice president on behalf of the people.
1868 Amendment 14	The number of Representatives shall be determined by the number of male citizens, 21 years and older, minus those who are denied voting rights for criminal convictions.
1869 Amendment 15	Citizens of the U.S. cannot be denied the right to vote due to race or color.
1913 Amendment 17	Each state will elect two senators to serve for six years each.
1920 Amendment 19	Citizens of the U.S. cannot be denied the right to vote due to sex.
1961 Amendment 23	The District of Columbia will appoint electors to vote for president and vice president.
1962 Amendment 24	Citizens of the U.S. cannot be denied the right to vote for failure to pay taxes.
1971 Amendment 26	Voting age is lowered to 18 years old.

2. Divide a large class into pairs or groups of three. Give each team a set of event strips and a blank time line (or have them draw a time line).

3. Have learners put the events in chronological order and create a time line.

4. Review the time line as a whole class. Discuss the events and the order in which they happened. Ask, "Does the order of events make sense?" For example, "Why was Amendment 15 approved so long before Amendment 19?"

SUGGESTIONS

• Use this as a race. Put event strips in envelopes or hand them out facedown. Have learners begin at the same time and race to put the strips in order on a time line.

• Make the activity more challenging by leaving out some information. For example, leave out the dates and have learners look up when each amendment was approved. Or leave off what the amendment was about and have learners fill it in. This can be a good end-of-unit review activity or quiz.

Digital Literacy

To succeed on the computer-based GED test, adult learners must be comfortable applying basic digital literacy skills to test scenarios. By introducing and encouraging regular use of technology tools such as email, word processing software, online news sources, and social media, you can promote positive computing experiences that will help prepare your students to excel on the exam and beyond. This chapter outlines the specific digital literacy skills needed to navigate the computer-based GED test and presents strategies you can use to help your students gain confidence at the keyboard while developing these essential skills.

The Digital Literacy Skills That Test-Takers Need

The digital literacy skills required for computer-based tests are similar to those needed for common technology tasks such as browsing the Internet, typing an email, or completing an online form, but there are specific skills such as quick and accurate typing and mouse navigation that are particularly important for test-takers. Students who use digital technology—traditional or mobile—on a regular basis will benefit from work on the specific computing skills listed below. Practicing these skills will help them complete the GED test efficiently. Students who are not yet comfortable with technology may be motivated to improve their general digital literacy level by working on these skills. The skills test-takers need are the same as the skills we all need today to succeed in academic and professional settings:

- using the mouse and keyboard to give the computer commands,

- scrolling down a page,

- reading text on the computer screen,

- dragging and dropping answers into a graph or chart,

- navigating between tabs to read passages,

- using navigation arrows to move between test questions,

- typing fill-in-the-blank, short answer, and extended responses into text fields,

- working with interactive images such as graphs with plot points,

- manipulating an on-screen digital calculator,

- cutting, copying, and pasting within typed response areas, and

- selecting answers or symbols from drop-down menus.

Preparing for Instruction

Many GED instructors (and students) already use technology in their personal or professional lives on a regular basis. Do you use email, texting, social media, or other technology to communicate professionally? Do you access articles, podcasts, or videos online to learn about new subjects or stay up to date on current events? Do you use online library catalogs or other databases to find materials and information? If you answered yes to any of these questions, you are probably fairly comfortable with technology.

Digital tasks have become so embedded in our daily practices that we often complete these processes on autopilot. We rarely pause to recognize the skills we are using, yet many of these skills can be adapted and applied in the computer-based testing environment. As you consider how to explicitly teach your students these skills for the test, think about the digital tasks you complete on a daily basis. Your challenge is to break each relevant task down into a series of small, concrete steps that you can easily explain and demonstrate to students in the context of the test questions.

What if you are not comfortable with technology? How can you prepare yourself to teach digital literacy skills to students? Begin by visiting the GED Testing Service Educator Website [www.gedtestingservice.com/educators]. The website includes online item samplers that represent the types of questions that students will encounter on the test. Explore the various question formats. Think about how you would approach each technology-enhanced problem. Do not focus on the academic skills and content knowledge; instead focus on the digital steps you need to take to complete each task.

For example, to write an extended response, you will probably have to:

1. Click between page tabs to read the question and supporting text on the screen.

2. Use the keyboard to type your response into the text field.

3. Use the shift key to capitalize the first letter in the sentence.

4. Use undo, backspace, or delete to make changes in what you write.

5. Use the enter key to start a new paragraph.

6. Click and drag the mouse to select a sentence.

7. Use CTRL + C and CTRL + V to cut and paste the sentence to a different place in your response.

8. Use special characters such as quotation marks and other punctuation to complete your response.

Once you understand how you would complete each type of test item, you will have a greater awareness of the digital literacy skills needed to navigate the test, and you will be better equipped to teach your students.

Digital Literacy Curricula

While most of the activities in this chapter explicitly address the specific digital literacy skills students need to succeed on the computer-based GED test, keep in mind that there are many ways you can encourage students to use technology in and out of the classroom, cultivating positive computing experiences and reducing the stress associated with tests. One strategy is to supplement GED curriculum with face-to-face or online self-paced digital literacy instruction. There are several examples of free online curricula that can be used to assess and build essential skills.

The following examples are appropriate for pre-GED and GED-level students:

Microsoft Digital Literacy

Microsoft's digital literacy curricula cover a broad range of topics from elementary computing skills to technical training for products such as MS Office. Courses are available on three levels: basic, standard, and advanced, and students can either complete the courses online or download the courses for offline completion.

www.microsoft.com/about/corporatecitizenship/citizenship/giving/programs/up/digitalliteracy/default.mspx

Northstar Digital Literacy Project

These free self-paced online modules can be used to assess adult learners' skill levels in six primary areas: Basic Computer Use, Internet, Windows Operating System, Mac OS, Email, and Word Processing (MS Word).

www.spclc.org/programs/digital-literacy-standards

Arlington Education and Employment Program (REEP) Reepworld

These interactive multimedia online exercises for students include supporting resources and curricula for instructors and tutors.

www.reepworld.org

REEP Technology Curriculum

These lessons focus on basic computer skills, word processing skills, Internet navigation skills, and email.

www.apsva.us/cms/lib2/VA01000586/Centricity/Domain/74/reepcurriculum/techcurriculum.html

Work and Technology Modules

These lessons work on several skills. One of these is the ability to use interactive forms, including job applications and cover letters.

www.apsva.us/cms/lib2/VA01000586/Centricity/Domain/74/reepcurriculum/lessonplanindex.html#work

Goodwill Community Foundation (GCF) Learn Free

This site includes thousands of self-paced learning modules on a wide variety of academic and life skills topics, including computer skills and digital literacy, as well as basic literacy and ESL (in the reading section). Start by clicking on the Technology button. You'll find many interactive lessons, including two that teach people how to connect cables to their computer and how to use a mouse. GCF also offers free online moderated courses on subjects including software use (e.g., MS Office).

www.gcflearnfree.org

Goodwill Community Foundation Learn Free—Spanish Version: www.gcfaprendelibre.org

For additional digital literacy curricula, stand-alone lessons, and resources, visit the Federal Digital Literacy Portal at www.digitalliteracy.gov.

Activity 62

Guided Tour of an Instructional Website

PURPOSE

To build students' confidence by exploring an instructional website.

METHOD

1. Note: This activity requires computers with Internet access.

2. Select a free instructional website such as GCF Learn Free (www.gcflearnfree.org) or one of the other sites listed in this chapter. Choose a site that students can access and use in class or on their own.

3. Explore the site before class, to become familiar with the navigation and website features.

4. Identify the features, online learning modules, or activities that you want students to use. Create a checklist of these items. Print a copy of the checklist for each student.

5. Preview the website for students using a projector, smart board, or screen share. Show students how to navigate the website and demonstrate the appropriate activities. Allow students to ask questions.

6. Hand out the checklist of activities. Ask students to find and explore each item on the list.

    Example checklist for GCF Learn Free:

    a. Find the About Us section and review it.

    b. Click on the Technology topic button.

        • Click on Computer Basics and review the topics available. Pick a lesson or video topic to explore.

    c. Click on the Math topic button.

        • Click on Decimals and Percents and review the topics available. Pick a lesson or video topic to explore.

    d. Click on Take a Free Online Class and review the topics available. Find the class catalog and open it to review the full list of classes.

    e. Wild card: Pick a section of the website to explore that is not listed above.

7. When students have completed the checklist, come back together as a class for Q & A. Give students time to ask questions about the website. Then ask them to share what they liked and disliked about the website. Have them describe the features they explored on their own. Ask them how they might use the website in the future.

Activity 63

Open Computer Lab

PURPOSE

To give students time to freely explore resources on the computer with support from instructors.

METHOD

1. Note: This activity requires computers with Internet access.

2. Prepare for the open computer lab by asking in advance what students want to practice or learn to do on the computer.

3. Based on the students' responses, prepare a short list of resources (e.g., high interest websites or software) for students to explore.

4. If you have many students and computers, recruit instructors or tutors to help in the lab. Students who are frequent computer users may also help guide new users.

5. Explain to the other instructors that this is an open lab and students are free to explore and practice skills on their own, within reason.

6. Post or distribute a list of suggested free resources.

7. Answer questions, troubleshoot technology problems, enforce computer lab rules, and guide students as they get comfortable using the computers.

SUGGESTIONS

•   Start the open lab with a brief introduction to the recommended resources using a projector, smart board, or screen sharing program so everyone can follow along.

•   Extend this activity with a teach-back session at the end where students will have one minute to share a website they discovered or something they learned.

•   If your class uses a learning management system (LMS) or secure social network, explain to students how they can post links and summaries of their findings during or after the session.

Activity 64

Computer Games: Seriously Fun

PURPOSE

To practice mouse and keyboard skills with computer games.

METHOD

1. Note: This activity requires computers with Internet access.

2. Select an online game or interactive activity that incorporates skills students will need for the GED test, such as dragging and dropping or typing. Find a free website that will give students practice with those skills.

    Examples:

Use a free typing practice program like Sense Lang MY Text (www.sense-lang.org) that allows the instructor to customize the text the students will practice typing. Copy and paste a passage from a news or literature website into the MY Text program. Students will be prompted to type the text of the passage word by word. They will be timed and tested for accuracy. Tip: If you do not have time to set up the MY Text option for every student, Sense Lang also includes several pre-loaded generic and BBC News-based typing lessons. You can also ask more advanced students to locate, copy, and paste text into the program on their own.

Use a site like Math Playground (www.mathplayground.com) to practice many of the math subjects that appear on the GED test. The wide variety of games on this website give students the opportunity to practice skills like dragging and dropping or plotting points on a graph.

The ReadWriteThink Letter Generator walks students through the process of creating a business or personal letter using text fields and "continue" buttons. Use this program to draft an invitation to graduation!

SUGGESTION

If many students are playing the same game, you can make this activity fun and provide incentive by offering awards for teams or individuals for the highest points, most improved, most persistent, etc. Create some healthy competition for the classroom!

Note: Many free games are funded by advertisers and may include content that is not appropriate for the classroom. Monitor use during class, and instruct students not to click on external links.

Activity 65

Using a Digital Calculator

PURPOSE

To use product videos and tutorials to practice with the TI-30XS digital calculator.

METHOD

1. Note: This activity requires computers with Internet access.

2. Prepare for the activity by exploring the GED Testing Service website for educators (www.gedtestingservice.com). View the fact sheet and online demonstration for the TI-30XS calculator that is used on the GED test.

3. Select several math practice problems that may require a calculator. Collect a variety of problems that will use different functions like percents, fractions, and exponents.

4. Present the calculator demonstration video to the class or choose classroom activities from Atomic Learning at www.atomiclearning.com/ti30xs.

5. After students view the demonstration or tutorial, have them practice using the calculator. A handheld version of the calculator is available for sale at New Readers Press and from other vendors. The handheld version works exactly like the onscreen calculator. Students may benefit from holding and practicing with the handheld calculator. Or you can purchase emulator software to practice with the onscreen version. More information on the emulator is available at the Atomic Learning website listed above.

6. After the students complete the practice problems, come together as a class to discuss any challenges or successes the students experienced with the digital calculator simulator.

Activity 66

Improving Words per Minute on Typed Responses

PURPOSE

To practice typing and keyboarding skills and improve typing speed.

METHOD

1. Note: This activity requires computers with Internet access.

2. Select a free typing practice website to share with your students. Choose from the examples listed in this chapter or find your own using a search engine like Google.

3. Familiarize yourself with the program and what it does. For example, www.TypingTest.com and www.sense-lang.org measure words per minute, adjusted for keystroke errors.

4. Find or create a video playlist of keyboarding skills relevant to your students' skill levels. For example, the Expert Village channel on YouTube offers a typing skills video series that covers the following topics:

   a. keys on the keyboard

   b. using caps lock and shift

   c. typing numbers

   d. typing a full sentence

   e. hand and finger placement

   f. proper posture

   g. memorizing keys

   Note that some typing practice websites also include useful tutorials that can be used in place of or in addition to online videos.

5. Show students how to access the typing practice program and set guidelines for the length of the test (time limit and number of characters). Ask students to complete one exercise as a baseline. Document the results.

6. Give students time to independently explore the typing tutorials and videos. Allow them to ask questions. Then ask students to complete additional exercises in the typing practice program.

7. Observe students' performance. Suggest specific tips or tutorials to reduce errors and increase typing speed.

SUGGESTION

Create a chart to display words-per-minute achievements. Create cards for all the students with names or pictures. Put the student cards up on the chart to mark their typing test results in words per minute. As their results improve, celebrate their accomplishments by moving them up or across the chart.

Insert Symbols: Happy π Day!

PURPOSE

To use special character menus to practice inserting symbols in text.

METHOD

1. Note: This activity requires computers or mobile devices.

2. This activity can be done on a computer or on mobile devices such as cell phones or tablets. Students can share a device, if necessary. Students do not have to actually send the messages they will be creating.

3. Prepare by demonstrating how to open a symbol menu. Many cell phones have symbol menus. You can also demonstrate using MS Word or an email program. You can find examples online in device manuals or product tutorial videos.

4. Create a list of equations or sentences that require using symbols or punctuation marks and either post the list or distribute a handout.

   Examples:

   - It's 3/14. Happy π Day!

   - Everything is 50% off!

   - $\sqrt{16} = 4 = 2 \times 2$

   - $\sqrt[3]{36} \geq 2x$

5. Remind students that rules for classroom behavior and responsible computing also apply when using mobile devices.

6. Explain the purpose of the activity: to select a symbol from a menu and insert it into text.

7. Discuss the list of messages and the symbols used. Students can add other messages and equations to the list.

8. Ask students to use the keyboards on their handheld mobile devices or on the computer to type the messages using numbers, symbols, and punctuation from symbol menus. Ask them not to use slide-out or detached keyboards, because they do not have hidden menus.

9. Answer questions and check message accuracy.

Activity 68

Bookmarking Digital Resources

PURPOSE

To practice bookmarking or flagging items for future review.

METHOD

1. Note: This activity requires computers with Internet access.

2. One of the most common methods of flagging web-based content for future use is bookmarking. This activity uses a social bookmarking tool called Delicious which allows users to create bookmark lists that they can access from any computer or mobile device that is connected to the Internet. Most browser-based bookmark lists are tied to a specific computer.

3. Prepare for the exercise by creating a free Delicious bookmarking or flagging account for your class. Go to www.delicious.com and follow the instructions for creating the account. Everyone in your class may have access to the same account.

4. Once you create your class account, you can bookmark sites in one of two ways: Add the Delicious Bookmarklet tool to your browser window by dragging the Bookmarklet button into the browser menu. Click on the Add to Delicious button when you are on a website you wish to flag. Or log in to Delicious, click on Add Link, and copy and paste the link to the web resource in the text field that appears. Either way the flagged resources will appear in the links section in your Delicious class account when you or your students log in to the website.

5. Demonstrate the bookmarking process for students. Ask students to suggest a test topic and choose a related key word. For example, if students suggest science as a core topic, you might choose a key term such as GED practice life science.

6. Go to a search engine, and enter the key words.

7. Review the search engine results, and select three resources that you would like to save. (Many search engines give you the option to filter your results to include websites, images only, and even YouTube videos to help you find exactly what you are looking for.)

8. Add the top results to your Delicious bookmark list using one of the methods listed in step 2.

9. Now ask students to log in to the class account at www.delicious.com on their own computers. Have them complete additional resource searches independently or in pairs. Ask them to share their findings by adding links to the class account.

Extended Response Items

PURPOSE

To practice typing and word processing skills needed for the computer-based extended response items.

METHOD

1. Note: This activity requires computers with Internet access.

2. Model an extended response item by selecting a web-based text passage for students to read. Supply a prompt or question for them to write about.

3. If you want to model a split-screen test item, open a blank word processing document on the right side of the screen, and open the reading passage on the left side. Set this up for students, or talk them through setting it up themselves.

4. Explain that students will practice writing an extended response on the computer. Tell students that this is just a practice activity, but that you will time them. Explain that on the test, they will be allowed 45 minutes for an RLA extended response and 25 minutes for social studies. For practice, tell students when time is almost up and then when the time has expired. Allow students to finish, and keep track of how long it takes. With practice, they should learn to answer the questions within the allotted time. Students should already be familiar with the word processing skills they can use on the test. If they are just beginning to practice typing on computers, do not time them yet.

5. Using a projector, smart board, or screen sharing, model for students how to read the article(s) and begin typing their responses.

6. For students who need reading comprehension practice, you may wish to read the passage together, as a class. Ask volunteers to read aloud as others follow along.

7. Help students to use word processing skills, if necessary, while they type.

8. When the students have completed their responses, demonstrate how to save or print the essays so that they can review them later.

SUGGESTION

Some students will require support for this complex task. Ease them into this activity by first having them write out their responses by hand. Then they can practice typing their responses on the computer.

Spelling and Grammar Check

PURPOSE

To practice correcting spelling and grammar in context.

METHOD

1. Note: This activity requires computers with word processing software.

2. Provide students with a writing prompt or have them type an essay that they have already written.

3. When students are finished typing, demonstrate how to use a spelling and grammar check program to identify and correct errors. This feature is typically found in the Review menu.

4. Go through all the errors one at a time. Show students the suggested corrections. Explain that the program cannot tell whether they have written the correct word, so students will have to be careful. Show them that they need to look at the suggestions and choose the correct word or spelling. You may want to refer to the Editing Checklist in Appendix E for examples of errors to check for.

5. Now ask students to run the spelling and grammar check on their own responses.

6. Afterward, discuss the process. Ask what the students like and dislike about the spelling and grammar check feature, and discuss whether it was helpful during the editing process for the extended response question. Explain that they will need to check their own writing on the test, as this feature will not be available.

GED Assessment Targets

Reading Assessment Targets

Common Core Connection: R.2[1]	Range of Depth of Knowledge (DOK) Levels[2]
Determine central ideas or themes of texts and analyze their development; summarize the key supporting details and ideas.	

		Range of Depth of Knowledge (DOK) Levels[2]
R.2.1	Comprehend explicit details and main ideas in text.	**1-2**
R.2.2	Summarize details and ideas in text.	**2**
R.2.3	Make sentence level inferences about details that support main ideas.	**2-3**
R.2.4	Infer implied main ideas in paragraphs or whole texts.	**2-3**
R.2.5	Determine which detail(s) support(s) a main idea.	**1-3**
R.2.6	Identify a theme, or identify which element(s) in a text support a theme.	**1-3**
R.2.7	Make evidence-based generalizations or hypotheses based on details in text, including clarifications, extensions, or applications of main ideas to new situations.	**2-3**
R.2.8	Draw conclusions or make generalizations that require synthesis of multiple main ideas in text.	**2-3**
Common Core Connection: R.3		
Analyze how individuals, events, and ideas develop and interact over the course of a text.		
R.3.1	Order sequences of events in texts.	**1-2**

1 See the Common Core State Standards for English Language Arts and Literacy at www.corestandards.org for more information on the reference codes listed at the beginning of each Reading Assessment Target.

2 The Depth of Knowledge (DOK) levels correspond with Norman Webb's (University of Wisconsin) Depth of Knowledge model of cognitive complexity.

		Range of Depth of Knowledge (DOK) Levels
R.3.2	Make inferences about plot/sequence of events, characters/people, settings, or ideas in texts.	2
R.3.3	Analyze relationships within texts, including how events are important in relation to plot or conflict; how people, ideas, or events are connected, developed, or distinguished; how events contribute to theme or relate to key ideas; or how a setting or context shapes structure and meaning.	2-3
R.3.4	Infer relationships between ideas in a text (e.g., an implicit cause and effect, parallel, or contrasting relationship.	2-3
R.3.5	Analyze the roles that details play in complex literary or informational texts.	2-3
Common Core Connection: R.4.2; L.4.2		
Interpret words and phrases that appear frequently in texts from a wide variety of disciplines, including determining connotative and figurative meanings from context and analyzing how specific word choices shape meaning or tone.		
R.4.1/L.4.1	Determine the meaning of words and phrases as they are used in a text, including determining connotative and figurative meanings from context.	1-3
R.4.2/L.4.2	Analyze how meaning or tone is affected when one word is replaced with another.	2
R.4.3/L.4.3	Analyze the impact of specific words, phrases, or figurative language in text, with a focus on an author's intent to convey information or construct an argument.	2-3
Common Core Connection: R.5[1]		
Analyze the structure of texts, including how specific sentences or paragraphs relate to each other and the whole.		
R.5.1	Analyze how a particular sentence, paragraph, chapter, or section fits into the overall structure of a text and contributes to the development of the ideas.	2-3
R.5.2	Analyze the structural relationship between adjacent sections of text (e.g., how one paragraph develops or refines a key concept or how one idea is distinguished from another).	2-3
R.5.3	Analyze transitional language or signal words (words that indicate structural relationships, such as *consequently*, *nevertheless*, *otherwise*) and determine how they refine meaning, emphasize certain ideas, or reinforce an author's purpose.	2
R.5.4	Analyze how the structure of a paragraph, section, or passage shapes meaning, emphasizes key ideas, or supports an author's purpose.	2-3

		Range of Depth of Knowledge (DOK) Levels
Common Core Connection: R.6		
Determine an author's purpose or point of view in a text and explain how it is conveyed and shapes the content and style of a text.		
R.6.1	Determine an author's point of view or purpose of a text.	1-2
R.6.2	Analyze how the author distinguishes his or her position from that of others or how an author acknowledges and responds to conflicting evidence or viewpoints.	2-3
R.6.3	Infer an author's implicit as well as explicit purposes based on details in text.	2
R.6.4	Analyze how an author uses rhetorical techniques to advance his or her point of view or achieve a specific purpose (e.g., analogies, enumerations, repetition and parallelism, juxtaposition of opposites, qualifying statements).	2-3
Common Core Connection: R.8		
Delineate and evaluate the argument and specific claims in a text, including the validity of the reasoning as well as the relevance and sufficiency of the evidence.		
R.8.1	Delineate the specific steps of an argument the author puts forward, including how the argument's claims build on one another.	2-3
R.8.2	Identify specific pieces of evidence an author uses in support of claims or conclusions.	1-3
R.8.3	Evaluate the relevance and sufficiency of evidence offered in support of a claim.	2-3
R.8.4	Distinguish claims that are supported by reasons and evidence from claims that are not.	2-3
R.8.5	Assess whether the reasoning is valid; identify fallacious reasoning in an argument and evaluate its impact.	2-3
R.8.6	Identify an underlying premise or assumption in an argument and evaluate the logical support and evidence provided.	2-3
Common Core Connection: R.7 & R.9		
Analyze how two or more texts address similar themes or topics		
R.9.1/R.7.1	Draw specific comparisons between two texts that address similar themes or topics or between information presented in different formats (e.g., between information presented in text and information or data summarized in a table or time line).	2-3
R.9.2	Compare two passages in similar or closely related genres that share ideas or themes, focusing on similarities and/or differences in perspective, tone, style, structure, purpose, or overall impact.	2-3

		Range of Depth of Knowledge (DOK) Levels
R.9.3	Compare two argumentative passages on the same topic that present opposing claims (either main or supporting claims) and analyze how each text emphasizes different evidence or advances a different interpretation of facts.	2-3
R.7.2	Analyze how data or quantitative and/or visual information extends, clarifies, or contradicts information in text, or determine how data supports an author's argument.	2-3
R.7.3	Compare two passages that present related ideas or themes in different genres or formats (e.g., a feature article and an online FAQ, or fact sheet) in order to evaluate differences in scope, purpose, emphasis, intended audience, or overall impact when comparing.	2-3
R.7.4	Compare two passages that present related ideas or themes in different genres or formats in order to synthesize details, draw conclusions, or apply information to new situations.	2-3

Writing Assessment Targets

Common Core Connections: R.1[3]		Range of Depth of Knowledge (DOK) Levels[4]
W.1	Determine the details of what is explicitly stated and make logical inferences or valid claims that square with textual evidence.	1-3
Common Core Connection: W.1, W.2, and W.4		
W.2	Produce an extended analytic response in which the writer introduces the idea(s) or claim(s) clearly; creates an organization that logically sequences information; develops the idea(s) or claim(s) thoroughly with well-chosen examples, facts, or details from the text; and maintains a coherent focus.	2-3
Common Core Connection: W.5 and L.1, L.2, and L.3		
W.3	Write clearly and demonstrate sufficient command of standard English conventions.[5]	1-2

3 See the Common Core State Standards for English Language Arts and Literacy at www.corestandards.org for more information on the reference codes listed at the beginning of each Writing Assessment Target.

4 The Depth of Knowledge (DOK) levels correspond with Norman Webb's (University of Wisconsin) Depth of Knowledge model of cognitive complexity.

5 "Sufficient command of standard English conventions" is meant to signal that the assessment would seek "mostly correct use" by students, not "total correctness." See RLA Extended Response Scoring Rubric, Trait 3 (page 171) for more information.

Language Assessment Targets

Common Core Connection: L.1[6]	Range of Depth of Knowledge (DOK) Levels[7]
Demonstrate command of the conventions of standard English grammar and usage when writing or speaking.	
L.1.1 Edit to correct errors involving frequently confused words and homonyms, including contractions (passed, past; two, too, to; there, their, they're; knew, new; it's, its).	**1-2**
L.1.2 Edit to correct errors in straightforward subject-verb agreement.	**1-2**
L.1.3 Edit to correct errors in pronoun usage, including pronoun-antecedent agreement, unclear pronoun references, and pronoun case.	**1-2**
L.1.4 Edit to eliminate nonstandard or informal usage (e.g., correctly use "try to win the game" instead of "try and win the game").	**1-2**
L.1.5 Edit to eliminate dangling or misplaced modifiers or illogical word order (e.g., correctly use "to meet almost all requirements" instead of "to almost meet all requirements").	**1-2**
L.1.6 Edit to ensure parallelism and proper subordination and coordination.	**1-2**
L.1.7 Edit to correct errors in subject-verb or pronoun antecedent agreement in more complicated situations (e.g., with compound subjects, interceding phrases, or collective nouns).	**1-2**
L.1.8 Edit to eliminate wordiness or awkward sentence construction.	**1-2**
L.1.9 Edit to ensure effective use of transitional words, conjunctive adverbs, and other words and phrases that support logic and clarity.	**1-2**
Common Core Connection: L.2	
Demonstrate command of the conventions of standard English capitalization and punctuation when writing.	
L.2.1 Edit to ensure correct use of capitalization (e.g., proper nouns, titles, and beginnings of sentences).	**1-2**
L.2.2 Edit to eliminate run-on sentences, fused sentences, or sentence fragments.	**1-2**
L.2.3 Edit to ensure correct use of apostrophes with possessive nouns.	**1-2**
L.2.4 Edit to ensure correct use of punctuation (e.g., commas in a series or in appositives and other non-essential elements, end marks, and appropriate punctuation for clause separation).	**1-2**

6   See the Common Core State Standards for English Language Arts and Literacy at www.corestandards.org for more information on the reference codes listed at the beginning of each Language Assessment Target.

7   The Depth of Knowledge (DOK) levels correspond with Norman Webb's (University of Wisconsin) Depth of Knowledge model of cognitive complexity.

Mathematical Reasoning Assessment Targets

Common Core State Standards References[8]		Quantitative Problem Solving Assessment Targets Content Indicators	Range of Depth of Knowledge (DOK)[9]
	Q.1	**Apply number sense concepts, including ordering rational numbers, absolute value, multiples, factors, and exponents.**	
4.NF.2; 6.NS.6; 6.NS.7	Q.1.a	Order fractions and decimals, including on a number line.	
6.NS.4	Q.1.b	Apply number properties involving multiples and factors, such as using the least common multiple, greatest common factor, or distributive property to rewrite numeric expressions.	1-2
8.EE.1; N-RN.2	Q.1.c	Apply rules of exponents in numerical expressions with rational exponents to write equivalent expressions with rational exponents.	1-2
6.NS.7; 7.NS.1	Q.1.d	Identify absolute value or a rational number as its distance from 0 on the number line and determine the distance between two rational numbers on the number line, including using the absolute value of their difference.	1-2
	Q.2	**Add, subtract, multiply, divide, and use exponents and roots of rational, fraction, and decimal numbers.**	
7.NS.1; 7.NS.2	Q.2.a	Perform addition, subtraction, multiplication, and division on rational numbers.	1-2
8.EE.2; N-RN.2	Q.2.b	Perform computations and write numerical expressions with squares and square roots of positive rational numbers.	1-2
8.EE.2; N-RN.2	Q.2.c	Perform computations and write numerical expressions with cubes and cube roots of rational numbers.	1-2
7.NS.2	Q.2.d	Determine when a numerical expression is undefined.	2
7.NS.3; 7.EE.3; 8.EE.4; N-Q.1	Q.2.e	Solve one-step or multi-step real-world arithmetic problems involving the four operations with rational numbers, including those involving scientific notation.	1-2
	Q.3	**Calculate and use ratios, percents, and scale factors.**	
6.RP.3; 7.RP.1; G-MG.2	Q.3.a	Compute unit rates. Examples include but are not limited to: unit pricing, constant speed, persons per square mile, BTUs per cubic foot.	1-2

8 See the Common Core State State Standards for Mathematics at www.corestandards.org for more information on the reference codes listed in the column.

9 The Depth of Knowledge (DOK) levels correspond to Norman Webb's (University of Wisconsin) Depth of Knowledge model for cognitive complexity.

Common Core State Standards References		Quantitative Problem Solving Assessment Targets Content Indicators	Range of Depth of Knowledge (DOK)
7.G.1	Q.3.b	Use scale factors to determine the magnitude of a size change. Convert between actual drawings and scale drawings.	1-2
	Q.4	**Calculate dimensions, perimeter, circumference, and area of two-dimensional figures.**	
7.G.6	Q.4.a	Compute the area and perimeter of triangles and rectangles. Determine side lengths of triangles and rectangles when given area or perimeter.	1-2
7.G.4	Q.4.b	Compute the area and circumference of circles. Determine the radius or diameter when given area or circumference	1-2
6.EE.2; 7.G.6	Q.4.c	Compute the perimeter of a polygon. Given a geometric formula, compute the area of a polygon. Determine side lengths of the figure when given the perimeter or area.	1-2
6.EE.2; 7.G.6; 8.G.9	Q.4.d	Compute perimeter and area of 2D composite geometric figures, which could include circles, given geometric formulas as needed.	1-2
8.G.7	Q.4.e	Use the Pythagorean Theorem to determine unknown side lengths in a right triangle.	1-2
	Q.5	**Calculate dimensions, surface area, and volume of three-dimensional figures.**	
6.EE.2; 7.G.6; 8.G.9	Q.5.a	When given geometric formulas, compute volume and surface area of rectangular prisms. Solve for side lengths or height when given volume or surface area.	1-2
6.EE.2; 7.G.6; 8.G.9	Q.5.b	When given geometric formulas, compute volume and surface area of cylinders. Solve for height, radius, or diameter when given volume or surface area.	1-2
6.EE.2; 7.G.6; 8.G.9	Q.5.c	When given geometric formulas, compute volume and surface area of right prisms. Solve for side lengths or height when given volume or surface area.	1-2
6.EE.2; 7.G.6; 8.G.9	Q.5.d	When given geometric formulas, compute volume and surface area of right pyramids and cones. Solve for side lengths, height, radius, or diameter when given volume or surface area.	1-2
6.EE.2; 8.G.9	Q.5.e	When given geometric formulas, compute volume and surface area of spheres. Solve for radius or diameter when given the surface area.	1-2
6.EE.2; 8.G.9	Q.5.f	Compute surface area and volume of composite 3D geometric figures, given geometric formulas as needed.	1-2

Common Core State Standards References		Quantitative Problem Solving Assessment Targets Content Indicators	Range of Depth of Knowledge (DOK)
	Q.6	**Interpret and create data displays.**	
7.RP.2; 3.MD.3	Q.6.a	Represent, display, and interpret categorical data in bar graphs or circle graphs.	**1-2**
S-ID.1	Q.6.b	Represent, display, and interpret data involving one-variable plots on the real number line including dot plots, histograms, and box plots.	**1-2**
8.SP.1	Q.6.c	Represent, display, and interpret data involving two variables in tables and the coordinate plane including scatter plots and graphs.	**1-2**
	Q.7	**Calculate and use mean, median, mode, and weighted average.**	
6.SP.3; S-MD.2	Q.7.a	Calculate the mean, median, mode, and range. Calculate a missing data value, given the average and all the missing data values but one, as well as calculating the average, given the frequency counts of all the data values, and calculating a weighted average.	**1-2**
	Q.8	**Utilize counting techniques and determine probabilities.**	
S-CP.9	Q.8.a	Use counting techniques to solve problems and determine combinations and permutations.	**1-2**
7.SP.7; 7.SP.8; S-CP.1; S-CP.2	Q.8.b	Determine the probability of simple and compound events.	**1-2**

Common Core State Standards References[10]		Algebraic Problem Solving Assessment Targets Content Indicators	Range of Depth of Knowledge (DOK)[11]
	A.1	**Write, evaluate, and compute with expressions and polynomials.**	
7.EE.1	A.1.a	Add, subtract, factor, multiply and expand linear expressions with rational coefficients.	**1-2**
6.EE.2	A.1.b	Evaluate linear expressions by substituting integers for unknown quantities.	**1-2**
6.EE.2; 6.EE.6	A.1.c	Write linear expressions as part of word-to-symbol translations or to represent common settings.	**1-2**

10 See the Common Core State State Standards for Mathematics at www.corestandards.org for more information on the reference codes listed in the column.

11 The Depth of Knowledge (DOK) levels correspond to Norman Webb's (University of Wisconsin) Depth of Knowledge model for cognitive complexity.

Common Core State Standards References		Algebraic Problem Solving Assessment Targets Content Indicators	Range of Depth of Knowledge (DOK)
A-APR.1	A.1.d	Add, subtract, multiply polynomials, including multiplying two binomials, or divide factorable polynomials.	1-2
6.EE.2	A.1.e	Evaluate polynomial expressions by substituting integers for unknown quantities.	1-2
A-SSE.2; A-SSE.3; A-SSE.4	A.1.f	Factor polynomial expressions.	1-2
6.EE.2; 6.EE.6	A.1.g	Write polynomial expressions as part of word-to-symbol translations or to represent common settings.	1-2
6.EE.3	A.1.h	Add, subtract, multiply, and divide rational expressions.	1-2
6.EE.2	A.1.i	Evaluate rational expressions by substituting integers for unknown quantities.	1-2
6.EE.2; 6.EE.6	A.1.j	Write rational expressions as part of word-to-symbol translations or to represent common settings.	1-2
	A.2	**Write, manipulate, and solve linear equations.**	
7.EE.4; 8.EE.7; A-REI.3	A.2.a	Solve one-variable linear equations with rational number coefficients, including equations whose solutions require expanding expressions using the distributive property and collecting like terms or equations with coefficients represented by letters.	1-2
7.EE.4; A-CED.1; A-CED.2	A.2.b	Solve real-world problems involving linear equations.	1-2
6.EE.6; A-CED.1; A-CED.2	A.2.c	Write one-variable and multi-variable linear equations to represent context.	1-2
8.EE.6; A-REI.6	A.2.d	Solve a system of two simultaneous linear equations by graphing, substitution, or linear combination. Solve real-world problems leading to a system of linear equations.	1-2
	A.3	**Write, manipulate, solve, and graph linear inequalities.**	
A-REI.3	A.3.a	Solve linear inequalities in one variable with rational number coefficients.	1-2
6.EE.8; 7.EE.4	A.3.b	Identify or graph the solution to a one-variable linear inequality on a number line.	1-2
7.EE.4; A-CED.1; A-CED.2	A.3.c	Solve real-world problems involving inequalities.	1-2

Common Core State Standards References		Algebraic Problem Solving Assessment Targets Content Indicators	Range of Depth of Knowledge (DOK)
6.EE.2; A-CED.1; A-CED.2	A.3.d	Write linear inequalities in one variable to represent context.	1–2
	A.4	**Write, manipulate, and solve quadratic equations.**	
A-REI.4	A.4.a	Solve quadratic equations in one variable with rational coefficients and real solutions, using appropriate methods (e.g., quadratic formula, completing the square, factoring, inspection).	1–2
A-CED.1	A.4.b	Write one-variable quadratic equations to represent context .	1–2
	A.5	**Connect and interpret graphs and functions.**	
6.NS.6	A.5.a	Locate points in the coordinate plane.	1
8.F.4	A.5.b	Determine the slope of a line from a graph, equation, or table.	1–2
8.EE.5	A.5.c	Interpret unit rate as the slope in a proportional relationship.	2
A-CED.2; F-IF.7	A.5.d	Graph two-variable linear equations.	1–2
8.F.3; 8.F.5; F-IF.5	A.5.e	For a function that models a linear or nonlinear relationship between two quantities, interpret key features of graphs and tables in terms of quantities, and sketch graphs showing key features of graphs and tables in terms of quantities, and sketch graphs showing key features given a verbal description of the relationship. Key features include: intercepts; intervals where the function is increasing, decreasing, positive, or negative; relative maximums and minimums; symmetries; end behavior, and periodicity.	1–2
	A.6	**Connect coordinates, lines, and equations.**	
A-CED.2	A.6.a	Write the equation of a line with a given slope through a given point.	1–2
A-CED.2	A.6.b	Write the equation of a line passing through two given distinct points.	2
G-GPE.5	A.6.c	Use slope to identify parallel and perpendicular lines and to solve geometric problems.	1–2
	A.7	**Compare, represent, and evaluate functions.**	
8.EE.5	A.7.a	Compare two different proportional relationships represented in different ways. Examples include but are not limited to: compare a distance-time graph to a distance-time equation to determine which of two moving objects has a greater speed.	2

Common Core State Standards References		Algebraic Problem Solving Assessment Targets Content Indicators	Range of Depth of Knowledge (DOK)
8.F.1; F-IF.1	A.7.b	Represent or identify a function in a table or graph as having exactly one output (one element in the range) for each input (each element in the domain).	1-2
F-IF.2	A.7.c	Evaluate linear and quadratic functions for values in their domain when represented using function notation.	1-2
8.F.2; F-IF.9	A.7.d	Compare properties of two linear or quadratic functions, each represented in a different way (algebraically, numerically in tables, graphically, or by verbal descriptions). Examples include but are not limited to: given a linear function represented by a table of values and a linear function represented by an algebraic expression, determine which function has the greater rate of change.	2

References[12]	Mathematical Practices	Range of Depth of Knowledge (DOK)[13]
M1, M3, M4, M5 N2, N5, N6, N8	**MP.1 Building Solution Pathways and Lines of Reasoning**	
	Search for and recognize entry points for solving a problem.	1-2
	Plan a solution pathway or outline a line of reasoning.	1-3
	Select the best solution pathway, according to given criteria.	2-3
	Recognize and identify missing information that is required to solve a problem.	1-2
	Select the appropriate mathematical technique(s) to use in solving a problem or a line of reasoning.	1-3
M2, M4 N2, N3	**MP.2 Abstracting Problems**	
	Represent real-world problems algebraically.	1-2
	Represent real-world problems visually.	1-2
	Recognize the important and salient attributes of a problem.	2-3

12 The GED® Mathematics Practices (MP#) are derived from the Common Core State Standards Math Practices (M#) and National Council of Teachers of Mathematics' Principles and Standards for School Mathematics (N#).

13 The Depth of Knowledge (DOK) levels correspond to Norman Webb's (University of Wisconsin) Depth of Knowledge model of cognitive complexity.

References	Mathematical Practices	Range of Depth of Knowledge (DOK)
M3 N7, N9	**MP.3 Furthering Lines of Reasoning**	
	Build steps of a line of reasoning or solution pathway, based on previous step or givens.	1-3
	Complete the lines of reasoning of others.	1-3
	Improve or correct a flawed line of reasoning.	2-3
M2, M4, M6 N1, N2, N9	**MP.4 Mathematical Fluency**	
	Manipulate and solve arithmetic expressions.	1-2
	Transform and solve algebraic expressions.	1-2
	Display data or algebraic expressions graphically.	1-2
M3 N7	**MP.5 Evaluating Reasoning and Solution Pathways**	
	Recognize flaws in others' reasoning.	2-3
	Recognize and use counterexamples.	2-3
	Identify the information required to evaluate a line of reasoning.	2-3

Science Assessment Targets

References to Common Core State Standards and Framework for K-12 Science Education[14]	Science Practices	Range of Depth of Knowledge (DOK) levels[15]
	SP.1 Comprehending Scientific Presentations	
R2, R8, P8, M2, M6	SP.1.a Understand and explain textual scientific presentations.	1-3
R4, L4, P8, M2, M4, M6	SP.1.b Determine the meaning of symbols, terms, and phrases as they are used in scientific presentations.	2

14 The GED® Science Practices are derived from The Common Core State Standards for ELA and Literacy (2010), The Common Core State Standards for Mathematics (2010), and the National Research Council's A Framework for K-12 Science Education: Practices, Crosscutting Concepts and Core Ideas.

15 The Depth of Knowledge (DOK) levels correspond to Norman Webb's (University of Wisconsin) Depth of Knowledge model of cognitive complexity.

References to Common Core State Standards and Framework for K-12 Science Education	Science Practices	Range of Depth of Knowledge (DOK) levels
S-ID, 8.SP, P8, M2, M4, M6	SP.1.c Understand and explain non-textual scientific presentations.	2
	SP.2 Investigation Design (Experimental and Observational)	
R8, P3, P4, M4	SP.2.a Identify possible sources of error and alter the design of an investigation to ameliorate that error.	2-3
R2, R5, W5, P1, P8, M, M4, M8	SP.2.b Identify and refine hypotheses for scientific investigations.	2-3
R8, R9, P2, P5, M3, M4	SP.2.c Identify the strengths and weaknesses of one or more scientific investigation (i.e., experimental or observational) designs.	2-3
W7, 3.MD, P3, P5, M4, M8	SP.2.d Design a scientific investigation.	1-3
R5, P2, P4, M4	SP.2.e Identify and interpret independent and dependent variables in scientific investigations.	2-3
	SP.3 Reasoning from Data	
R1, P7	SP.3.a Cite specific textual evidence to support a finding or conclusion.	2-3
R1, R2, R3, P1, P6, P7, M3, M4, M7, M8	SP.3.b Reason from data or evidence to a conclusion.	2-3
R1, R3, P4, M3, M4, M7, M8	SP.3.c Make a prediction based upon data or evidence.	2-3
S-CP, 7.SP, P4, P5, M4, M7, M8	SP.3.d Use sampling techniques to answer scientific questions.	2-3
	SP.4 Evaluating Conclusions with Evidence	
R8, P4, P6, M3, M7, M8	SP.4.a Evaluate whether a conclusion or theory is supported or challenged by particular data or evidence.	2-3
	SP.5 Working with Findings	
R9, P2, P4, P6, M3, M7	SP.5.a Reconcile multiple findings, conclusions, or theories.	2-3
	SP.6 Expressing Scientific Information	
R7, W2, P8, M2, M4, M6	SP.6.a Express scientific information or findings visually.	2
R7, W2, P5, P8, M2, M4, M6	SP.6.b Express scientific information or findings numerically or symbolically.	1-2

References to Common Core State Standards and Framework for K-12 Science Education	Science Practices	Range of Depth of Knowledge (DOK) levels
R7, W2, P8, M2, M6	SP.6.c Express scientific information or findings verbally.	2-3
	SP.7 Scientific Theories	
R3, R5, L3, P1, P2, P7, M2, M4	SP.7.a Understand and apply scientific models, theories and processes.	2-3
P2, P5, M2, M4, M8	SP.7.b Apply formulas from scientific theories.	2
	SP.8 Probability & Statistics	
S-MD, S-ID, P4, P5, M4, M6	SP.8.a Describe a data set statistically.	1-2
7.SP, P5, M4, M6	SP.8.b Use counting and permutations to solve scientific problems.	1-2
7.SP, S-CP, P5, M4, M6	SP.8.c Determine the probability of events.	2

Science Content Topics Matrix

		Science Content Topics		
		Life Science (L) (40%)	Physical Science (P) (40%)	Earth and Space Science (ES) (20%)
Focusing Themes	**Human Health and Living Systems**	a. Human body and health b. Organization of life (structure and function of life) c. Molecular basis for heredity d. Evolution	a. Chemical properties and reactions related to human systems	a. Interactions between Earth's systems and living things
	Energy and Related Systems	e. Relationships between life functions and energy intake f. Energy flows in ecologic networks (ecosystems)	b. Conservation, transformation, and flow of energy c. Work, motion, and forces	b. Earth and its system components and interactions c. Structure and organization of the cosmos

Science Content Topics and Subtopics[16]

Life Science	
L.a	**Human Body and Health**
	L.a.1 Body systems (e.g., muscular, endocrine, nervous systems) and how they work together to perform a function (e.g., muscular and skeletal work to move the body)
	L.a.2 Homeostasis, feedback methods that maintain homeostasis (e.g., sweating to maintain internal temperature), and effects of changes in the external environment on living things (e.g., hypothermia, injury)
	L.a.3 Sources of nutrients (e.g., foods, symbiotic organisms) and concepts in nutrition (e.g., calories, vitamins, minerals)
	L.a.4 Transmission of disease and pathogens (e.g., airborne, bloodborne), effects of disease or pathogens on populations (e.g., demographics change, extinction), and disease prevention methods (e.g., vaccination, sanitation)
L.b	**Relationship Between Life Functions and Energy Intake**
	L.b.1 Energy for life functions (e.g., photosynthesis, respiration, fermentation)
L.c	**Energy Flows in Ecologic Networks (Ecosystems)**
	L.c.1 Flow of energy in ecosystems (e.g., energy pyramids), conservation of energy in an ecosystem (e.g., energy lost as heat, energy passed on to other organisms), and sources of energy (e.g., sunlight, producers, lower level consumer)
	L.c.2 Flow of matter in ecosystems (e.g., food webs and chains, positions of organisms in the web or chain) and the effects of change in communities or environments on food webs
	L.c.3 Carrying capacity, changes in carrying capacity based on changes in populations and environmental effects, and limiting resources necessary for growth
	L.c.4 Symbiosis (e.g., mutualism, parasitism, commensalism) and predator/prey relationships (e.g., changes in one population affecting another population)
	L.c.5 Disruption of ecosystems (e.g., invasive species, flooding, habitat destruction, desertification) and extinction (e.g., causes [human and natural] and effects)
L.d	**Organization of Life (Structure and Function of Life)**
	L.d.1 Essential functions of life (e.g., chemical reactions, reproduction, metabolism) and cellular components that assist the functions of life (e.g., cell membranes, enzymes, energy)
	L.d.2 Cell theory (e.g., cells come from cells, cells are the smallest unit of living things), specialized cells and tissues (e.g., muscles, nerves, etc.), and cellular levels of organization (e.g., cells, tissues, organs, systems)
	L.d.3 Mitosis, meiosis (e.g., process and purpose)

16 The GED® Science Content Topics are informed by the National Research Council's A Framework for K-12 Science Education: Practices, Crosscutting Concepts and Core Ideas 2011.

	Life Science
L.e	**Molecular Basis for Heredity**
	L.e.1 Central dogma of molecular biology, the mechanism of inheritance (e.g., DNA), and chromosomes (e.g., description, chromosome splitting during meiosis)
	L.e.2 Genotypes, phenotypes, and the probability of traits in close relatives (e.g., Punnett squares, pedigree charts)
	L.e.3 New alleles, assortment of alleles (e.g., mutations, crossing over), environmental altering of traits, and expression of traits (e.g., epigenetics, color points of Siamese cats)
L.f	**Evolution**
	L.f.1 Common ancestry (e.g., evidence) and cladograms (e.g., drawing, creating, interpreting)
	L.f.2 Selection (e.g., natural selection, artificial selection, evidence) and the requirements for selection (e.g., variation in traits, differential survivability)
	L.f.3 Adaptation, selection pressure, and speciation

	Physical Science
P.a	**Conservation, Transformation, and Flow of Energy**
	P.a.1 Heat, temperature, the flow of heat resulting in work, and the transfer of heat (e.g., conduction, convection)
	P.a.2 Endothermic and exothermic reactions
	P.a.3 Types of energy (e.g., kinetic, chemical, mechanical) and transformations between types of energy (e.g., chemical energy [sugar] to kinetic energy [motion of a body])
	P.a.4 Sources of energy (e.g., sun, fossil fuels, nuclear) and the relationships between different sources (e.g., levels of pollution, amount of energy produced)
	P.a.5 Types of waves, parts of waves (e.g., frequency, wavelength), types of electromagnetic radiation, transfer of energy by waves, and the uses and dangers of electromagnetic radiation (e.g., radio transmission, UV light, and sunburns)
P.b	**Work, Motion, and Forces**
	P.b.1 Speed, velocity, acceleration, momentum, and collisions (e.g., inertia in a car accident, momentum transfer between two objects)
	P.b.2 Force, Newton's Laws, gravity, acceleration due to gravity (e.g., freefall, law of gravitational attraction), mass, and weight
	P.b.3 Work, simple machines (types and functions), mechanical advantages (force, distance, and simple machines), and power

Physical Science	
P.c	**Chemical Properties and Reactions Related to Living Systems**
	P.c.1 Structure of matter
	P.c.2 Physical and chemical properties, changes of state, and density
	P.c.3 Balancing chemical equations and different types of chemical equations, conservation of mass in balanced chemical equations, and limiting reactants
	P.c.4 Parts in solutions, general rules of solubility (e.g., hotter solvents allow more solute to dissolve), saturation, and the differences between weak and strong solutions

Earth and Space Science	
ES.a	**Interactions between Earth's Systems and Living Things**
	ES.a.1 Interactions of matter between living and non-living things (e.g., cycles of matter) and the location, uses, and dangers of fossil fuels
	ES.a.2 Natural hazards (e.g., earthquakes, hurricanes, etc.) their effects (e.g., frequency, severity, and short- and long-term effects), and mitigation thereof (e.g., dikes, storm shelters, building practices)
	ES.a.3 Extraction and use of natural resources, renewable vs. non-renewable resources and sustainability
ES.b	**Earth and Its System Components and Interactions**
	ES.b.1 Characteristics of the atmosphere, including its layers, gases, and their effects on the Earth and its organisms, including climate change
	ES.b.2 Characteristics of the oceans (e.g., saltwater, currents, coral reefs) and their effects on Earth and organisms
	ES.b.3 Interactions between Earth's systems (e.g., weathering caused by wind or water on rock, wind caused by high/low pressure and Earth rotation, etc.)
	ES.b.4 Interior structure of the Earth (e.g., core, mantle, crust, tectonic plates) and its effects (e.g., volcanoes, earthquakes, etc.) and major landforms of the Earth (e.g., mountains, ocean basins, continental shelves, etc.)
ES.c	**Structures and Organization of the Cosmos**
	ES.c.1 Structures in the universe (e.g., galaxies, stars, constellations, solar systems), the age and development of the universe, and the age and development of stars (e.g., main sequence, stellar development, deaths of stars [black hole, white dwarf])
	ES.c.2 Sun, planets, and moons (e.g., types of planets, comets, asteroids), the Earth's motion, and the interactions within the Earth's solar system (e.g., tides, eclipses)
	ES.c.3 The age of the Earth, including radiometrics, fossils, and landforms

Social Studies Assessment Targets

References to Common Core State Standards, NCSS and NSH[17]	Social Studies Practices	Range of Depth of Knowledge (DOK) levels[18]
R.1, R.8	**SSP.1 Drawing Conclusions and Making Inferences**	
	a. Determine the details of what is explicitly stated in primary and secondary sources and make logical inferences or valid claims based on evidence.	2-3
	b. Cite or identify specific evidence to support inferences or analyses of primary and secondary sources, attending to the precise details of explanations or descriptions of a process, event, or concept.	1-3
R.2, NCSS Literacy Skills	**SSP.2 Determining Central Ideas, Hypotheses, and Conclusions**	
	a. Determine the central ideas or information of a primary or secondary source document, corroborating or challenging conclusions with evidence.	1-3
	b. Describe people, places, environments, processes, and events, and the connections between and among them.	2-3
R.3, R.8	**SSP.3 Analyzing Events and Ideas**	
	a. Identify the chronological structure of a historical narrative and sequence steps in a process.	1-2
	b. Analyze in detail how events, processes, and ideas develop and interact in a written document; determine whether earlier events caused later ones or simply preceded them.	2-3
	c. Analyze cause-and-effect relationships and multiple causation, including action by individuals, natural and societal processes, and the influence of ideas.	2-3
	d. Compare differing sets of ideas related to political, historical, economic, geographic, or societal contexts; evaluate the assumptions and implications inherent in differing positions.	2-3
R.4.2, L.4.2.	**SSP.4 Interpreting Meaning of Symbols, Words, and Phrases**	
	a. Determine the meaning of words and phrases as they are used in context, including vocabulary that describes historical, political, social, geographic, and economic aspects of social studies.	1-3

17 The GED® Social Studies practices are derived from the Common Core State Standards for ELA and Literacy (2010), the Common Core State Standards for Mathematics (2010), NCSS National Curriculum Standards for Social Studies: A Framework for Teaching, Learning, and Assessment (NCSS Literacy Skills) (2010), and National Standards for History Revised Edition (1996).

18 The Depth of Knowledge (DOK) levels correspond with Norman Webb's (University of Wisconsin) Depth of Knowledge model of cognitive complexity.

References to Common Core State Standards, NCSS and NSH	Social Studies Practices	Range of Depth of Knowledge (DOK) levels
	SSP.5 Analyzing Purpose and Point of View	
R.6, NSH 3.F	a. Identify aspects of a historical document that reveal an author's point of view or purpose (e.g., loaded language, inclusion or avoidance of particular facts).	2
	b. Identify instances of bias or propagandizing.	2-3
	c. Analyze how a historical context shapes an author's point of view.	2-3
	d. Evaluate the credibility of an author in historical and contemporary political discourse.	2-3
	SSP.6 Integrating Content Presented in Different Ways	
R.9.1, R.7.1, R.7.2, Q7: 7.RP, 3.MD.3, S-ID.1, 8.SP.1, S-ID.6, S-ID.7, NSH 2	a. Integrate quantitative or technical analysis (e.g., charts, research data) with qualitative analysis in print or digital text.	2-3
	b. Analyze information presented in a variety of maps, graphic organizers, tables, and charts and in a variety of visual sources such as artifacts, photographs, political cartoons.	2-3
	c. Translate quantitative information expressed in words in a text into visual form (e.g., table or chart); translate information expressed visually or mathematically into words.	1-3
	SSP.7 Evaluating Reasoning and Evidence	
R.8, NSH 3.E	a. Distinguish among fact, opinion, and reasoned judgment in a primary or secondary source document.	2-3
	b. Distinguish between unsupported claims and informed hypotheses grounded in social studies evidence.	2-3
	SSP.8 Analyzing Relationships between Texts	
R.9, R.7	a. Compare treatments of the same social studies topic in various primary and secondary sources, noting discrepancies between and among the sources.	2-3
	SSP.9 Writing Analytic Response to Source Texts[19]	
R.1, W.1, W.2, W.4, W.5, L.1, L.2, L.4	a. Produce writing that develops the idea(s), claim(s), and/or argument(s) thoroughly and logically, with well-chosen examples, facts, or details from primary and secondary source documents.	2-3

19 The Extended Response writing task will require test-takers to apply a range of social studies practices; however, the practices under SSP.9 will be of primary importance in the writing task, and these practices will only be assessed through the writing task.

References to Common Core State Standards, NCSS and NSH	Social Studies Practices	Range of Depth of Knowledge (DOK) levels
	b. Produce writing that introduces the idea(s) or claim(s) clearly; creates an organization that logically sequences information; and maintains a coherent focus.	2-3
	c. Write clearly and demonstrate sufficient command of standard English conventions.	1-2
Q7: 7.RP, 3.MD.3, S-ID.1, 8.SP.1, S-ID.6, S-ID.7	**SSP.10 Reading and Interpreting Graphs, Charts, and Other Data Representation**	
	a. Interpret, use, and create graphs (e.g., scatterplot, line, bar, circle) including proper labeling. Predict reasonable trends based on the data (e.g., do not extend trend beyond a reasonable limit).	2-3
	b. Represent data on two variables (dependent and independent) on a graph; analyze and communicate how the variables are related.	2-3
	c. Distinguish between correlation and causation.	1-3
Q8: 6.SP.3, S-MD.2, 6.SP.2, 6.SP.5, S-ID.2, S-ID.3, S-ID.4, S-ID.9	**SSP.11 Measuring the Center of a Statistical Dataset**	
	a. Calculate the mean, median, mode, and range of a dataset.	1

Social Studies Content Topics

Focusing Themes	Social Studies Topic Matrix			
	CG: Civics and Government (50%)	USH: U.S. History (20%)	E: Economics (15%)	G: Geography and the World (15%)
I. Development of Modern Liberties and Democracy	a. Types of modern and historical governments b. Principles that have contributed to development of American constitutional democracy c. Structure and design of United States government d. Individual rights and civic responsibilities	a. Key historical documents that have shaped American constitutional government b. Revolutionary and Early Republic Periods c. Civil War & Reconstruction d. Civil Rights Movement	a. Key economic events that have shaped American government and policies b. Relationship between political and economic freedoms	a. Development of classical civilizations
II. Dynamic Responses in Societal Systems	e. Political parties, campaigns, and elections in American politics f. Contemporary public policy	e. European population of the Americas f. World Wars I & II g. The Cold War h. American foreign policy since 9/11	c. Fundamental economic concepts d. Microeconomics and macroeconomics e. Consumer economics f. Economic causes and impacts of wars g. Economic drivers of exploration and colonization h. Scientific and Industrial Revolutions	b. Relationships between the environment and societal development c. Borders between peoples and nations d. Human migration

Social Studies Content Topics and Subtopics

Civics and Government	
CG.a	**Types of modern and historical governments**
	CG.a.1 Direct democracy, representative democracy, parliamentary democracy, presidential democracy, monarchy, and other types of government that contributed to the development of American constitutional democracy
CG.b	**Principles that have contributed to development of American constitutional democracy**
	CG.b.1 Natural rights philosophy
	CG.b.2 Popular sovereignty and consent of the governed
	CG.b.3 Constitutionalism
	CG.b.4 Majority rule and minority rights
	CG.b.5 Checks and balances
	CG.b.6 Separation of powers
	CG.b.7 Rule of law
	CG.b.8 Individual rights
	CG.b.9 Federalism
CG.c	**Structure and design of United States government**
	CG.c.1 Structure, powers, and authority of the federal executive, judicial, and legislative branches
	CG.c.2 Individual governmental positions (e.g., president, speaker of the house, cabinet secretary, etc.)
	CG.c.3 Major powers and responsibilities of the federal and state governments
	CG.c.4 Shared powers
	CG.c.5 The amendment process
	CG.c.6 Governmental departments and agencies
CG.d	**Individual rights and civic responsibilities**
	CG.d.1 The Bill of Rights
	CG.d.2 Personal and civil liberties of citizens
CG.e	**Political parties, campaigns, and elections in American politics**
	CG.e.1 Political parties
	CG.e.2 Interest groups
	CG.e.3 Political campaigns, elections, and the electoral process
CG.f	**Contemporary public policy**

TEACHING ADULTS: A GED® TEST RESOURCE BOOK

United States History		
USH.a	**Key historical documents that have shaped American constitutional government**	
	USH.a.1 Key documents and the context and ideas that they signify (e.g., Magna Carta, Mayflower Compact, Declaration of Independence, United States Constitution, Martin Luther King, Jr.'s Letter from the Birmingham Jail, landmark decisions of the United States Supreme Court, and other key documents)	
USH.b	**Revolutionary and early Republic periods**	
	USH.b.1 Revolutionary War	
	USH.b.2 War of 1812	
	USH.b.3 George Washington	
	USH.b.4 Thomas Jefferson	
	USH.b.5 Articles of Confederation	
	USH.b.6 Manifest Destiny	
	USH.b.7 U.S. Indian Policy	
USH.c	**Civil War and Reconstruction**	
	USH.c.1 Slavery	
	USH.c.2 Sectionalism	
	USH.c.3 Civil War amendments	
	USH.c.4 Reconstruction policies	
USH.d	**Civil rights**	
	USH.d.1 Jim Crow laws	
	USH.d.2 Women's suffrage	
	USH.d.3 Civil Rights Movement	
	USH.d.4 Plessy vs. Ferguson and Brown vs. Board of Education	
	USH.d.5 Warren Court decisions	
USH.e	**European settlement and population of the Americas**	

United States History		
USH.f	**World Wars I & II**	
	USH.f.1 Alliance system	
	USH.f.2. Imperialism, nationalism, and militarism	
	USH.f.3 Russian Revolution	
	USH.f.4 Woodrow Wilson	
	USH.f.5 Treaty of Versailles and League of Nations	
	USH.f.6 Neutrality Acts	
	USH.f.7 Isolationism	
	USH.f.8 Allied and Axis Powers	
	USH.f.9 Fascism, Nazism, and totalitarianism	
	USH.f.10 The Holocaust	
	USH.f.11 Japanese-American internment	
	USH.f.12 Decolonization	
	USH.f.13 GI Bill	
USH.g	**The Cold War**	
	USH.g.1 Communism and capitalism	
	USH.g.2 NATO and the Warsaw Pact	
	USH.g.3 U.S. maturation as an international power	
	USH.g.4 Division of Germany, Berlin Blockade and Airlift	
	USH.g.5 Truman Doctrine	
	USH.g.6 Marshall Plan	
	USH.g.7 Lyndon B. Johnson and The Great Society	
	USH.g.8 Richard Nixon and the Watergate scandal	
	USH.g.9 Collapse of U.S.S.R. and democratization of Eastern Europe	
USH.h	**American foreign policy since 9/11**	

Economics	
E.a	**Key economic events that have shaped American government and policies**
E.b	**Relationship between political and economic freedoms**
E.c	**Fundamental economic concepts**
	E.c.1 Markets
	E.c.2 Incentives
	E.c.3 Monopoly and competition
	E.c.4 Labor and capital
	E.c.5 Opportunity cost
	E.c.6 Profit
	E.c.7 Entrepreneurship
	E.c.8 Comparative advantage
	E.c.9 Specialization
	E.c.10 Productivity
	E.c.11 Interdependence
E.d	**Microeconomics and macroeconomics**
	E.d.1 Supply, demand, and price
	E.d.2 Individual choice
	E.d.3 Institutions
	E.d.4 Fiscal and monetary policy
	E.d.5 Regulation and costs of government policies
	E.d.6 Investment
	E.d.7 Government and market failures
	E.d.8 Inflation and deflation
	E.d.9 GDP
	E.d.10 Unemployment
	E.d.11 Tariffs
E.e	**Consumer economics**
	E.e.1 Types of credit
	E.e.2 Savings and banking
	E.e.3 Consumer credit laws
E.f	**Economic causes and impacts of wars**
E.g	**Economic drivers of exploration and colonization**
E.h	**Scientific and Industrial Revolutions**

Geography		
G.a	**Development of classical civilizations**	
G.b	**Relationships between the environment and societal development**	
	G.b.1 Nationhood and statehood	
	G.b.2 Sustainability	
	G.b.3 Technology	
	G.b.4 Natural resources	
	G.b.5 Human changes to the environment	
G.c	**Borders between peoples and nations**	
	G.c.1 Concepts of region and place	
	G.c.2 Natural and cultural diversity	
	G.c.3 Geographic tools and skills	
G.d	**Human migration**	
	G.d.1 Immigration, emigration, and diaspora	
	G.d.2 Culture, cultural diffusion, and assimilation	
	G.d.3 Population trends and issues	
	G.d.4 Rural and urban settlement	

Extended Response Scoring Rubrics

RLA Extended Response Scoring Rubric

Score	Description
Trait 1: Creation of Arguments and Use of Evidence	
2	• generates text-based argument(s) and establishes a purpose that is connected to the prompt • cites relevant and specific evidence from source text(s) to support argument (may include a few irrelevant pieces of evidence or unsupported claims) • analyzes the issue and/or evaluates the validity of the argumentation within the source texts (e.g., distinguishes between supported and unsupported claims, makes reasonable inferences about underlying premises or assumptions, identifies fallacious reasoning, evaluates the credibility of sources, etc.)
1	• generates an argument and demonstrates some connection to the prompt • cites some evidence from source text(s) to support argument (may include a mix of relevant and irrelevant citations or a mix of textual and non-textual references) • partially analyzes the issue and/or evaluates the validity of the argumentation within the source texts; may be simplistic, limited, or inaccurate
0	• may attempt to create an argument OR lacks purpose or connection to the prompt OR does neither • cites minimal or no evidence from source text(s) (sections of text may be copied from source) • minimally analyzes the issue and/or evaluates the validity of the argumentation within the source texts; may completely lack analysis or demonstrate minimal or no understanding of the given argument(s)

Non-scorable Responses (Score of 0/Condition Codes)
Response exclusively contains text copied from source text(s) or prompt
Response shows no evidence that test-taker has read the prompt or is off-topic
Response is incomprehensible
Response is not in English
Response has not been attempted (blank)

Score	Description
Trait 2: Development of Ideas and Organizational Structure	
2	• contains ideas that are well developed and generally logical; most ideas are elaborated upon • contains a sensible progression of ideas with clear connections between details and main points • establishes an organizational structure that conveys the message and purpose of the response; applies transitional devices appropriately • establishes and maintains a formal style and appropriate tone that demonstrate awareness of the audience and purpose of the task • chooses specific words to express ideas clearly
1	• contains ideas that are inconsistently developed and/or may reflect simplistic or vague reasoning; some ideas are elaborated upon • demonstrates some evidence of a progression of ideas, but details may be disjointed or lacking connection to main ideas • establishes an organization structure that may inconsistently group ideas or is partially effective at conveying the message of the task; uses transitional devices inconsistently • may inconsistently maintain a formal style and appropriate tone to demonstrate an awareness of the audience and purpose of the task • may occasionally misuse words and/or choose words that express ideas in vague terms
0	• contains ideas that are insufficiently or illogically developed, with minimal or no elaboration on main ideas • contains an unclear or no progression of ideas; details may be absent or irrelevant to the main ideas • establishes an ineffective or no discernible organizational structure; does not apply transitional devices, or does so inappropriately • uses an informal style and/or inappropriate tone that demonstrates limited or no awareness of audience and purpose • may frequently misuse words, overuse slang, or express ideas in a vague or repetitious manner

Non-scorable Responses (Score of o/Condition Codes)

Response exclusively contains text copied from source text(s) or prompt

Response shows no evidence that test-taker has read the prompt or is off-topic

Response is incomprehensible

Response is not in English

Response has not been attempted (blank)

Score	Description
Trait 3: Clarity and Command of Standard English Conventions	

2	• demonstrates largely correct sentence structure and a general fluency that enhances clarity with specific regard to the following skills:
	
	  1. varied sentence structure within a paragraph or paragraphs
	
	  2. correct subordination, coordination, and parallelism
	
	  3. avoidance of wordiness and awkward sentence structures
	
	  4. usage of transitional words, conjunctive adverbs, and other words that support logic and clarity
	
	  5. avoidance of run-on sentences, fused sentences, or sentence fragments
	
	• demonstrates competent application of conventions with specific regard to the following skills:
	
	  1. frequently confused words and homonyms, including contractions
	
	  2. subject-verb agreement
	
	  3. pronoun usage, including pronoun antecedent agreement, unclear pronoun references, and pronoun case
	
	  4. placement of modifiers and correct word order
	
	  5. capitalization (e.g., proper nouns, titles, and beginnings of sentences)
	
	  6. use of apostrophes with possessive nouns
	
	  7. use of punctuation (e.g., commas in a series or in appositives and other non-essential elements, end marks, and appropriate punctuation for clause separation)
	
	• may contain some errors in mechanics and conventions, but they do not interfere with comprehension; overall, standard usage is at a level appropriate for on-demand draft writing

1	• demonstrates inconsistent sentence structure; may contain some repetitive, choppy, rambling, or awkward sentences that may detract from clarity; demonstrates inconsistent control over skills 1-5 as listed in the first bullet under Trait 3, Score Point 2 above • demonstrates inconsistent control of basic conventions with specific regard to skills 1–7 as listed in the second bullet under Trait 3, Score Point 2 above • may contain frequent errors in mechanics and conventions that occasionally interfere with comprehension; standard usage is at a minimally acceptable level of appropriateness for on-demand draft writing

Score	Description
Trait 3: Clarity and Command of Standard English Conventions	
1	• demonstrates consistently flawed sentence structure such that meaning may be obscured; demonstrates minimal control over skills 1-5 as listed in the first bullet under Trait 3, Score Point 2 above • demonstrates minimal control of basic conventions with specific regard to skills 1–7 as listed in the second bullet under Trait 3, Score Point 2 above • contains severe and frequent errors in mechanics and conventions that interfere with comprehension; overall, standard usage is at an unacceptable level for on-demand draft writing OR • response is insufficient to demonstrate level of mastery over conventions and usage

Because test-takers will be given only 45 minutes to complete Extended Response tasks, there is no expectation that a response should be completely free of convention or usage errors to receive a score of 2.

Non-scorable Responses (Score of 0/Condition Codes)

Response exclusively contains text copied from source text(s) or prompt

Response shows no evidence that test-taker has read the prompt or is off-topic

Response is incomprehensible

Response is not in English

Response has not been attempted (blank)

Social Studies Extended Response Scoring Rubric

Score	Description
Trait 1: Creation of Arguments and Use of Evidence	
2	• generates a text-based argument that demonstrates a clear understanding of the relationships among ideas, events, and figures as presented in the source text(s) and the historical contexts from which they are drawn • cites relevant and specific evidence from primary and secondary source text(s) that adequately supports an argument • is well-connected to both the prompt and the source text(s)
1	• generates an argument that demonstrates an understanding of the relationships among ideas, events, and figures as presented in the source text(s) • cites some evidence from primary and secondary source texts in support of an argument (may include a mix of relevant and irrelevant textual references) • is connected to both the prompt and the source text(s)
0	• may attempt to create an argument but demonstrates minimal or no understanding of the ideas, events, and figures presented in the source texts or the contexts from which these texts are drawn • cites minimal or no evidence from the primary and secondary source texts; may or may not demonstrate an attempt to create an argument • lacks connection either to the prompt or the source text(s)

Non-scorable Responses (Score of 0/Condition Codes)

Response exclusively contains text copied from source text(s) or prompt

Response demonstrates that the test-taker has read neither the prompt nor the source text(s)

Response is incomprehensible

Response is not in English

Response has not been attempted (blank)

Score	Description
Trait 2: Development of Ideas and Organizational Structure	
1	• Contains a sensible progression of ideas with understandable connections between details and main ideas • Contains ideas that are developed and generally logical; multiple ideas are elaborated upon • Demonstrates appropriate awareness of the task
0	• Contains an unclear or no apparent progression of ideas • Contains ideas that are insufficiently developed or illogical; just one idea is elaborated upon • Demonstrates no awareness of the task

Non-scorable Responses (Score of 0/Condition Codes)

Response exclusively contains text copied from source text(s) or prompt

Response demonstrates that the test-taker has read neither the prompt nor the source text(s)

Response is incomprehensible

Response is not in English

Response has not been attempted (blank)

Score	Description
Trait 3: Clarity and Command of Standard English Conventions	

1	• demonstrates adequate applications of conventions with specific regard to the following skills:
	
	  1. frequently confused words and homonyms, including contractions
	
	  2. subject-verb agreement
	
	  3. pronoun usage, including pronoun antecedent agreement, unclear pronoun references, and pronoun case
	
	  4. placement of modifiers and correct word order
	
	  5. capitalization (e.g., proper nouns, titles, and beginnings of sentences)
	
	  6. use of apostrophes with possessive nouns
	
	  7. use of punctuation (e.g., commas in a series or in appositives and other non-essential elements, end marks, and appropriate punctuation for clause separation)
	
	• demonstrates largely correct sentence structure with variance from sentence to sentence; is generally fluent and clear with specific regard to the following skills:
	
	  1. correct subordination, coordination, and parallelism
	
	  2. avoidance of wordiness and awkward sentence structures
	
	  3. usage of transitional words, conjunctive adverbs, and other words that support logic and clarity
	
	  4. avoidance of run-on sentences, fused sentences, or sentence fragments
	
	  5. standard usage at a level of formality appropriate for on-demand draft writing
	
	• may contain some errors in mechanics and conventions, but they do not interfere with understanding*

0	• demonstrates minimal control of basic conventions with specific regard to skills 1–7 as listed in the first bullet under Trait 3, Score Point 1 above • demonstrates consistently flawed sentence structure; minimal or no variance such that meaning may be obscured; demonstrates minimal control over skills 1–5 as listed in the second bullet under Trait 3, Score Point 1 above • contains severe and frequent errors in mechanics and conventions that interfere with comprehension OR • response is insufficient to demonstrate level of mastery over conventions and usage

* Because test-takers will be given only 25 minutes to complete Extended Response tasks, there is no expectation that a response should be completely free of conventions or usage errors to receive a score of 1.

Non-scorable Responses (Score of 0/Condition Codes)

Response exclusively contains text copied from source text(s) or prompt

Response demonstrates that the test-taker has read neither the prompt nor the source text(s)

Response is incomprehensible

Response is not in English

Response has not been attempted (blank)

Webb's Depth of Knowledge

English Language Arts[1]

Subject	Depth of Knowledge
English Language Arts	**Level 1**
	Requires students to recall, observe, question, or represent facts or simple skills or abilities. Requires only surface understanding of text, often verbatim recall or slight paraphrasing. Use conventions of standard English.
	Examples:
	• Support ideas by reference to specific details in text
	• Use dictionary to find meaning
	• Use punctuation marks correctly
	• Identify figurative language in passage
	• Identify correct spelling or meaning of words

1   The English Language Arts table is used with permission of Dr. Norman L. Webb from the University of Wisconsin Center for Educational Research.

Subject	Depth of Knowledge
English Language Arts	**Level 2** Requires processing beyond recall and observation. Requires both comprehension and subsequent processing of text. Involves ordering, classifying text as well as identifying patterns, relationships and main points. Connect ideas using simple organizational structures. Requires some scrutiny of text. Examples: • Use contextual clues to identify unfamiliar words • Predict logical outcome • Construct or edit compound or complex sentences • Identify and summarize main points • Apply knowledge of conventions of standard American English • Compose accurate summaries **Level 3** Requires students to go beyond text. Requires students to explain, generalize, and connect ideas. Involves inferencing, prediction, elaboration, and summary. Requires students to support positions using prior knowledge and to manipulate themes across passages. Students develop compositions with multiple paragraphs. Examples: • Determine effect of author's purpose on text elements • Summarize information from multiple sources • Critically analyze literature • Edit writing to produce logical progression • Compose focused, organized, coherent, purposeful prose **Level 4** Requires extended higher order processing. Typically requires extended time to complete task, but time spent not on repetitive tasks. Involves taking information from one text/passage and applying this information to a new task. May require generating hypotheses and performing complex analyses and connections among texts. Examples: • Analyze and synthesize information from multiple sources • Examine and explain alternative perspectives across sources • Describe and illustrate common themes across a variety of texts • Create compositions that synthesize, analyze, and evaluate

Mathematics[2]

Subject	Depth of Knowledge
Mathematics	**Level 1**
	Requires students to recall or observe facts, definitions, or terms. Involves simple one-step procedures. Involves computing simple algorithms (e.g., sum, quotient). Examples: • Recall or recognize a fact, term, or property • Represent in words, pictures, or symbols a math object or relationship • Perform routine procedure like measuring
	Level 2
	Requires students to make decisions of how to approach a problem. Requires students to compare, classify, organize, estimate, or order data. Typically involves two-step procedures. Examples: • Specify and explain relationships between facts, terms, properties, or operations • Select procedure according to criteria and perform it • Solve routine multiple-step problems
	Level 3
	Requires reasoning, planning, or use of evidence to solve problem or algorithm. May involve activity with more than one possible answer. Requires conjecture or restructuring of problems. Involves drawing conclusions from observations, citing evidence, and developing logical arguments for concepts. Uses concepts to solve non-routine problems. Examples: • Analyze similarities and differences between procedures • Formulate original problem given situation • Formulate mathematical model for complex situation

2 The Mathematics table is used with permission of Dr. Norman L. Webb from the University of Wisconsin Center for Educational Research.

Subject	Depth of Knowledge
Mathematics	**Level 4** Requires complex reasoning, planning, developing, and thinking. Typically requires extended time to complete problem, but time spent not on repetitive tasks. Requires students to make several connections and apply one approach among many to solve the problem. Involves complex restructuring of data, establishing and evaluating criteria to solve problems. Examples: • Apply mathematical model to illuminate a problem, situation • Conduct a project that specifies a problem, identifies solution paths, solves the problem, and reports results • Design a mathematical model to inform and solve a practical or abstract situation

Science[3]

Subject	Depth of Knowledge
Science	**Level 1 Recall & Reproduction** a. Recall or recognize a fact, term, definition, simple procedure (such as one step), or property b. Demonstrate a rote response c. Use a well-known formula d. Represent in words or diagrams a scientific concept or relationship e. Provide or recognize a standard scientific representation for simple phenomenon f. Perform a routine procedure, such as measuring length g. Perform a simple science process or a set procedure (like a recipe) h. Perform a clearly defined set of steps i. Identify, calculate, or measure NOTE: If the knowledge necessary to answer an item automatically provides the answer, it is a Level 1.

3 © Karin K. Hess, National Center of Assessment, Dover, NH. khess@nciea.org. Link: www.nciea.org/publications/ DOKscience_KH11.pdf

Subject	Depth of Knowledge
Science	**Level 2 Skills & Concepts** a. Specify and explain the relationship between facts, terms, properties, or variables b. Describe and explain examples and non-examples of science concepts c. Select a procedure according to specified criteria and perform it d. Formulate a routine problem given data and conditions e. Organize, represent, and compare data f. Make a decision as to how to approach the problem g. Classify, organize, or estimate h. Compare data i. Make observations j. Interpret information from a simple graph k. Collect and display data NOTE: If the knowledge necessary to answer an item does not automatically provide the answer, then the item is at least a Level 2. Most actions imply more than one step. NOTE: Level 3 is complex and abstract. If more than one response is possible, it is at least a Level 3 and calls for use of reasoning, justification, evidence, as support for the response. **Level 3 Strategic Thinking** a. Interpret information from a complex graph (such as determining features of the graph or aggregating data in the graph) b. Use reasoning, planning, and evidence c. Explain thinking (beyond a simple explanation or using only a word or two to respond) d. Justify a response e. Identify research questions and design investigations for a scientific problem f. Use concepts to solve nonroutine problems/more than one possible answer g. Develop a scientific model for a complex situation h. Form conclusions from experimental or observational data i. Complete a multi-step problem that involves planning and reasoning j. Provide an explanation of a principle k. Justify a response when more than one answer is possible l. Cite evidence and develop a logical argument for concepts m. Conduct a designed investigation n. Research and explain a scientific concept o. Explain phenomena in terms of concepts

Subject	Depth of Knowledge
Science	**Level 4 Extended Thinking**
	a. Select or devise approach among many alternatives to solve problem
	b. Based on provided data from a complex experiment that is novel to the student, deduct the fundamental relationship between several controlled variables
	c. Conduct an investigation, from specifying a problem to designing and carrying out an experiment to analyzing its data and forming conclusions
	d. Relate ideas within the content area or among content areas
	e. Develop generalizations of the results obtained and the strategies used and apply them to new problem situations
	NOTE: Level 4 activities often require an extended period of time for carrying out multiple steps; however, time alone is not a distinguishing factor if skills and concepts are simply repetitive over time.

Social Studies[4]

Subject	Depth of Knowledge
Social Studies	**Level 1 Recall of Information**
	a. Recall or recognition of: fact, term, concept, trend, generalization, event, or document
	b. Identify or describe features of places or people
	c. Identify key figures in a particular context meaning of words
	d. Describe or explain: who, what, where, when
	e. Identify specific information contained in maps, charts, tables, graphs, or drawings

4 © Karin K. Hess, National Center of Assessment, Dover, NH. khess@nciea.org. Link: www.nciea.org/publications/ DOKsocialstudies_KH08.pdf

Subject	Depth of Knowledge
Social Studies	**Level 2 Basic Reasoning** a. Describe cause-effect of particular events b. Describe or explain: how (relationships or results), why, points of view, processes, significance, or impact c. Identify patterns in events or behavior d. Categorize events or figures in history into meaningful groups e. Identify and summarize the major events, problem, solution, conflicts f. Distinguish between fact and opinion g. Organize information to show relationships h. Compare and contrast people, events, places, concepts i. Give examples and non-examples to illustrate an idea/concept **Level 3 Complex Reasoning** a. Explain, generalize, or connect ideas, using supporting evidence from a text/source b. Apply a concept in other contexts c. Make and support inferences about implied causes and effects d. Draw conclusion or form alternative conclusions e. Analyze how changes have affected people or places f. Use concepts to solve problems g. Analyze similarities and differences in issues or problems h. Propose and evaluate solutions i. Recognize and explain misconceptions related to concepts **Level 4 Extended Reasoning** a. Analyze and explain multiple perspectives or issues within or across time periods, events, or cultures b. Gather, analyze, organize, and synthesize information from multiple (print and non-print) sources c. Make predictions with evidence as support d. Plan and develop solutions to problems e. Given a situation/problem, research, define, and describe the situation/problem and provide alternative solutions f. Describe, define, and illustrate common social, historical, economic, or geographical themes and how they interrelate

Math Tools

Mathematics Symbol Selector

The 2014 GED® test on computer contains a tool called the "Symbol Selector," used in entering special mathematical symbols into fill-in-the-blank item types.

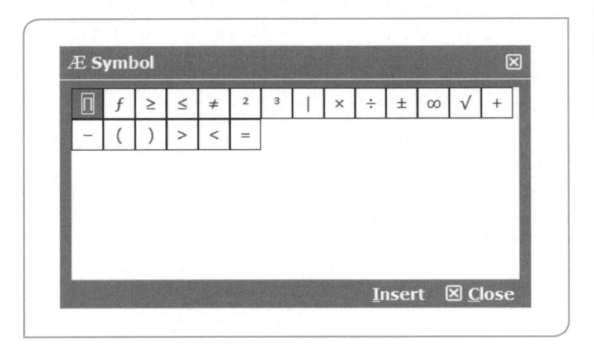

2014 GED® Test Mathematics Formula Sheet*

Area of a:

parallelogram	$A = bh$
trapezoid	$A = \frac{1}{2}h(b_1 + b_2)$

Surface Area and Volume of a:

rectangular/right prism	$SA = ph + 2B$	$V = Bh$
cylinder	$SA = 2\pi rh + 2\pi r^2$	$V = \pi r^2 h$
pyramid	$SA = \frac{1}{2}ps + B$	$V = \frac{1}{3}Bh$
cone	$SA = \pi rs + \pi r^2$	$V = \frac{1}{3}\pi r^2 h$
sphere	$SA = 4\pi r^2$	$V = \frac{4}{3}\pi r^3$

Algebra

slope of a line	$m = \dfrac{y_2 - y_1}{x_2 - x_1}$
slope-intercept form of the equation of a line	$y = mx + b$
point-slope form of the equation of a line	$y - y_1 = m(x - x_1)$
standard form of a quadratic equation	$y = ax^2 + bx + c$
quadratic formula	$x = \dfrac{-b \pm \sqrt{b^2 - 4ac}}{2a}$
Pythagorean Theorem	$a^2 + b^2 = c^2$
simple interest	$I = prt$ (I = interest, p = principal, r = rate, t = time)

* The Mathematics Formula Sheet contains basic, essential information necessary for answering items on the Mathematics Test. It will be available to test-takers during the entire Mathematics Test.

TI_30XS Calculator Reference Sheet

To perform basic arithmetic, enter numbers and operation symbols using the standard order of operations.

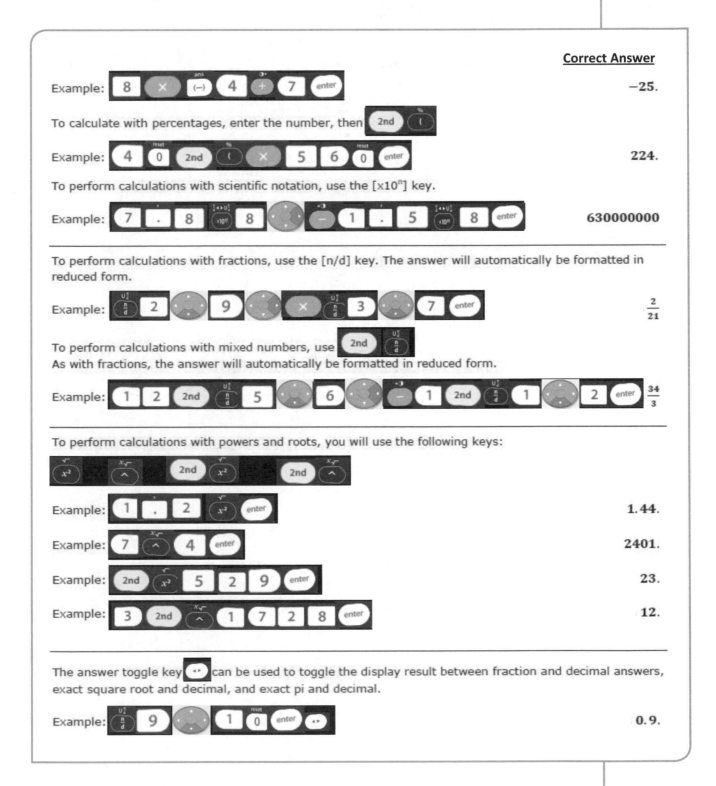

Correct Answer

Example: [8] [×] [(−)] [4] [+] [7] [enter]   −25.

To calculate with percentages, enter the number, then [2nd] [(]

Example: [4] [0] [2nd] [(] [×] [5] [6] [0] [enter]   224.

To perform calculations with scientific notation, use the [x10ⁿ] key.

Example: [7] [.] [8] [x10ⁿ] [8] [−] [1] [.] [5] [x10ⁿ] [8] [enter]   630000000

To perform calculations with fractions, use the [n/d] key. The answer will automatically be formatted in reduced form.

Example: [n/d] [2] [9] [×] [n/d] [3] [7] [enter] $\frac{2}{21}$

To perform calculations with mixed numbers, use [2nd] [n/d]
As with fractions, the answer will automatically be formatted in reduced form.

Example: [1] [2] [2nd] [n/d] [5] [6] [−] [1] [2nd] [n/d] [1] [2] [enter] $\frac{34}{3}$

To perform calculations with powers and roots, you will use the following keys:

[x²] [^] [2nd] [x²] [2nd] [^]

Example: [1] [.] [2] [x²] [enter]   1.44.

Example: [7] [^] [4] [enter]   2401.

Example: [2nd] [x²] [5] [2] [9] [enter]   23.

Example: [3] [2nd] [^] [1] [7] [2] [8] [enter]   12.

The answer toggle key [◄►] can be used to toggle the display result between fraction and decimal answers, exact square root and decimal, and exact pi and decimal.

Example: [n/d] [9] [1] [0] [enter] [◄►]   0.9.

Reproducible Worksheets

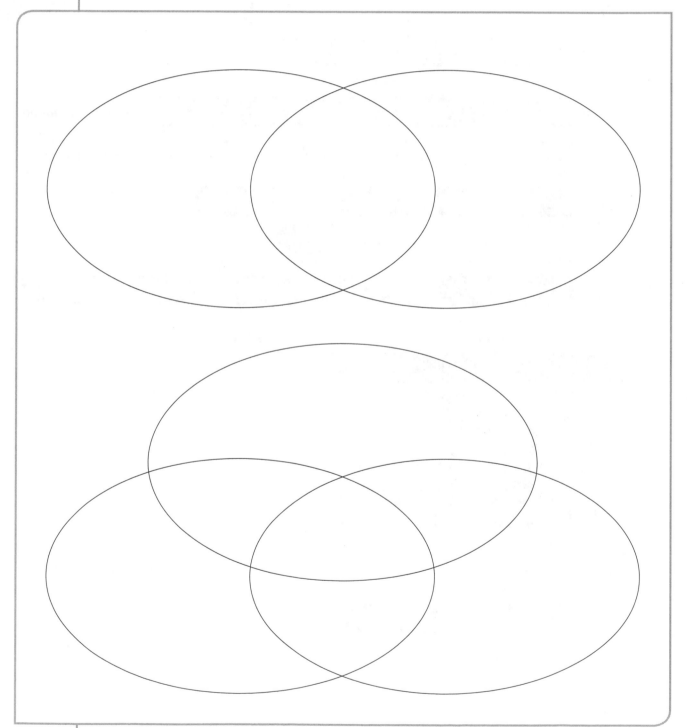

PROS	CONS

Main Idea:

Detail:

Detail:

Detail:

Detail:

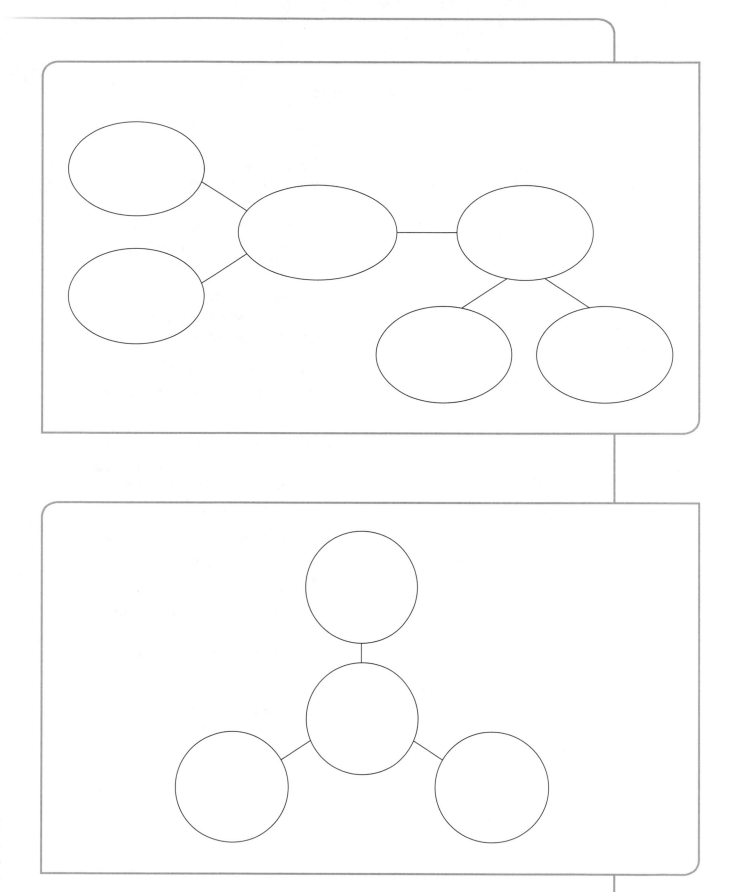

2014 GED Test Editing Checklist:

1. Did I use the right words?
    - Check frequently confused words and homonyms: passed, past; it's, its; all ready, already; two, to, too; there, their, they're; knew, new; lose, loose; suppose, supposed to; through, threw, through; who, whom; lie, lay; lead, led.

2. Do my subjects and verbs agree?
    - Check for singular or plural.

3. Do my pronouns (he, she, it, they) agree with their antecedents?
    - Check for singular or plural.

4. Are modifiers in the correct order?
    - Check for dangling or misplaced modifiers.

5. Are important words capitalized?
    - Check first word in a sentence, proper nouns, and titles.

6. Did I use apostrophes correctly?
    - Check for apostrophes in possessive nouns.
    - Check for no apostrophes in plural nouns.

7. Did I use commas correctly?
    - Check clauses, series, and appositives.

8. Does every sentence have an end mark?
    - Check for periods, question marks, and exclamation points.

9. Did I combine ideas and use conjunctions correctly?
    - Check for use of coordinating conjunctions (and, but, or, nor, for, so, yet).
    - Check for use of subordinating conjunctions (because, after, since, although, unless, until, etc.).

10. Are my ideas parallel?
    - Check that items compared or listed in a series have the same form.

11. Are my sentences clear and effective?
    - Check for repetitive words or awkward sentences.

12. Do my ideas follow a logical progression?
    - Check for use of transitional words and conjunctive adverbs to ensure logical order and clarity.

13. Did I correctly join or separate thoughts?
    - Check for run-on sentences or fused sentences.

14. Does every sentence contain a subject and verb?
    - Check for sentence fragments.

15. Did I select appropriate words?
    - Check for slang, nonstandard usage, informal words, or profanity.

Here is a list of math terms that GED students should be familiar with:

absolute value	elevation	manipulate	ray
acute	evaluate	matrix	quadratic equation
adjacent	event	mean	radius
arc	exponent	median	range
area	expression	midpoint	rate of change
average	factor	mode	ratio
binomial	formula	multiple	rational number
box plot	fraction	number properties	rectangle
chord	frequency	obtuse	right angle
circle	function	output	root
circumference	graph	percent	scale
coefficient	greatest common factor	perimeter	scalene
combination		periodicity	scientific notation
composite figure	histogram	permutation	slope
coordinate	inequality	perpendicular	square root
counterexample	input	plane	standard deviation
cube	integer	polygon	surface area
cube root	intercept	polynomial	symmetry
cylinder	interest	prism	translation
data	irrational number	probability	triangle
decimal	isosceles	proportion	unit rate
diameter	least common multiple	pyramid	unknown
dimension	like term	Pythagorean Theorem	variable
distributive property	linear expression	random	volume
dot plot			

Topic:

1

2

3

TEACHING ADULTS: A GED® TEST RESOURCE BOOK

Bibliography

Comings, J.P., Parrella, A., & Soricone, L. (1999). *Persistence Among Adult Basic Education Students in Pre-GED Classes.* Cambridge, MA: The National Center for the Study of Adult Learning and Literacy.

National Center for Learning Disabilities (2011). *The State of Learning Disabilities: Facts, Trends and Indicators.* New York, NY: National Center for Learning Disabilities.

Resnick, L.B. (Ed.) (1989). *Introduction, In Knowing, Learning and Instruction: Essays in Honor of Robert Glaser.* Hillsdale, NJ: Erlbaum.

Texas Center for the Advancement of Literacy & Learning (2010). *Texas Even Start Administrative Manual, Glossary of Adult Education Terms.* Houston, TX: Texas LEARNS. Retrieved from www-tcall.tamu.edu/docs/04esguide/glossary.htm

Thaiss, C. (1986). *Language Across the Curriculum in the Elementary Grades.* Urbana, Ill: ERIC Clearinghouse on Reading and Communication Skills and the National Council of Teachers of English.

Van Reusen, A.K., Bos, C., Schumaker, J.B., & Deshler, D.D. (1994). *Self-Advocacy Strategy for Education and Transition Planning.* Lawrence, KS: Edge Enterprises.

Zull, J.E. (2002). *The Art of Changing the Brain.* Sterling, VA: Stylus Publishing.